Saint Augustine of Hippo

Other Books in the
SkyLight Illuminations Series

Saint Augustine of Hippo

Selections from *Confessions* and Other Essential Writings— Annotated & Explained

Annotation by Joseph T. Kelley, PhD
Translation from the Augustinian Heritage Institute,
*The Works of Saint Augustine:
A Translation for the 21st Century*

Walking Together, Finding the Way®
SKYLIGHT PATHS®
PUBLISHING
Nashville, Tennessee

Saint Augustine of Hippo:
Selections from Confessions and Other Essential Writings—Annotated & Explained
2015 Quality Paperback Edition

Library of Congress Cataloging-in-Publication Data
Kelley, Joseph T., 1948–
   Saint Augustine of Hippo : selections from Confessions and other essential writings, annotated and explained / annotation by Joseph T. Kelley. — Quality paperback ed.
      p. cm. — (Skylight illuminations series)
"Translation from the Augustinian Heritage Institute, The Works of Saint Augustine: A Translation for the 21st Century."
   Includes bibliographical references and index.
   ISBN-13: 978-1-59473-282-9 (quality pbk.)
   ISBN-10: 1-59473-282-5 (quality pbk.)
   ISBN-13: 978-1-68336-277-7 (hc)

   1. Augustine, Saint, Bishop of Hippo. I. Augustine, Saint, Bishop of Hippo. Selections. English. 2010. II. Title.
   BR65.A9K395 2010
   270.2092—dc22

                                                                    2010004943

ISBN 978-1-59473-326-0 (eBook)

10 9 8 7 6 5 4 3 2
Manufactured in the United States of America
Cover design: Walter C. Bumford III, Stockton, Massachusetts, and Tim Holtz
Cover art: bas relief of Augustine, Cassago Brianza, Italy; Kevin Salemme, MFA (photo), Enrico Manfrini (sculpture).

SkyLight Paths Publishing is creating a place where people of different spiritual traditions come together for challenge and inspiration, a place where we can help each other understand the mystery that lies at the heart of our existence.

SkyLight Paths sees both believers and seekers as a community that increasingly transcends traditional boundaries of religion and denomination—people wanting to learn from each other, *walking together, finding the way.*

SkyLight Paths, "Walking Together, Finding the Way" and colophon are trademarks of LongHill Partners, Inc., registered in the U.S. Patent and Trademark Office.

Walking Together, Finding the Way®
Published by SkyLight Paths® Publishing
An Imprint of Turner Publishing Company
4507 Charlotte Avenue, Suite 100
Nashville, TN 37209
Tel: (615) 255-2665
www.skylightpaths.com

For Alina, Kasia, and Patryk

Et quo nisi deo plenus est qui plenus est dilectione?
De Trinitate VIII.5.12

Contents □

Part Three: Intent upon God   69

Part Four: While in the World   143

Preface □

Friendship was very important to Saint Augustine. He writes eloquently about it in his *Confessions* and in several letters and commentaries on scripture. His biographer, Peter Brown, remarks that Augustine seems never to be alone. Friends and family are always at hand, constant companions in mind and heart. For Augustine, the love of friends is one way in which we experience God, an important way into the reality of God who is love.

There are many friendships behind this book. First, there are my teachers and mentors. I mention particularly the Augustinian friars George Lawless and James Wenzel; and Donald Burt and John Rotelle (both of happy memory). Each one has enriched my life with his particular understanding of Saint Augustine and expertise in Augustinian studies. Together, their guidance, encouragement, and support have made possible this introductory text to Augustine's life and thought.

Beyond these four men, there is the wider community of friends known as the Order of Saint Augustine. Founded as part of the mendicant movement in thirteenth-century Europe, this Order draws its inspiration and rule of life from Augustine. Its members taught his theology in the medieval European universities. Augustinian friars continue to teach and preach throughout the world today. As a high school student in New York City, and later as a student at Villanova University, I benefited from their insistence on academic excellence and moral development. For a number of years I was a member of the Order. My life has been influenced and enriched by its spiritual and communal traditions, and many Augustinian friars are still among my closest friends.

My faculty colleagues at Merrimack College have been an extension of that Augustinian friendship, especially those who, over the past decade, have worked side by side with me in the Center for Augustinian Study and Legacy. I count these long associations among the greatest gifts of my life. In addition, I have been privileged to serve for many years on the board of the Augustinian Heritage Institute, which oversees the project of translating Augustine's works into a new English collection of his entire corpus. Patricia Lo, chair of the board, and the other members are dedicated to Augustinian scholarship and to advancing knowledge of Augustine's life and work. The translations of Augustine's writings in this anthology are taken mostly from the books in this series. I am indebted to the many scholars who have participated in this project and whose labors in the always difficult work of translation from Latin to English have made Augustine accessible to a new generation of readers.

Another friendship, begun in the mid-nineteenth century, is also responsible for this book. In the tiny Irish village of Rathbran, two young lads, John Fedigan and James Kelley, grew up as boyhood friends. The former immigrated to America, joined the Order of Saint Augustine, and became president of Villanova College (now Villanova University) and leader of the Order in the United States. The latter also found his way to Pennsylvania where he married and raised a family of six, supporting them through his trade as a tinsmith. He was my great-grandfather.

The friendship between these two immigrants continued in their new country, and together they helped the young Irish-Catholic community west of Philadelphia take root. It was also the beginning of a long association of my family, the Augustinian Order, and Villanova University. That acquaintance, four generations and over a century ago, has influenced my life in profound ways, both personally and professionally. This book is a fruit grown from the root of their friendship and from the love and support of my family.

More recent associations have also enriched my life and this text. Without the expert guidance and help from editors Emily Wichland and Michaela Powell of SkyLight Paths Publishing, this book would not have been possible. I am deeply grateful to them for their skill and support.

There is one more friendship to note: the one that may grow from our present association through this text. Though we may never meet in person, we meet within these pages as we explore together the life and writings of someone who lived over sixteen hundred years ago. Augustine would take delight in our exchange and admire our courage in trying to understand someone whose time, culture, language, and presuppositions are so different from our own. He would want us to engage his ideas with gusto, to disagree and challenge, to admit similarities and accept differences—all with openness to and respect for each other, as good friends do. He put it this way in an Introduction to one of his own books:

> Dear reader, whenever you are as certain about something as I am, go forward with me; whenever you stick equally fast, seek with me; whenever you notice that you have gone wrong come back to me; or that I have, call me back to you.... This covenant, both prudent and pious, I would wish to enter into in the sight of the Lord our God with all who read what I write....
>
> —*The Trinity* I.1.5

Our meeting in this text—you, Augustine, and I—is a kind of covenant, an agreement of the heart, even as we explore ideas of the mind. I hope this meeting is as rich and rewarding for you as my Augustinian friendships have been for me.

Introduction □

There is a charming legend about Saint Augustine. It tells how one day he was walking along the shore of the Mediterranean Sea, pondering the mystery of God. With each step on the sandy beach he strove for deeper understanding of the meaning of the Christian teaching of the Holy Trinity. A little child in the distance distracted the bishop from his meditation.

He saw the child walking back and forth from the water's edge to a spot on the beach. As Augustine approached, he saw that the child had a seashell for scooping up water from the sea. The little one carefully carried the shell, brimming with water, to a small hole in the sand and poured the salty contents into the hole. Then back to the sea for more water to repeat the process over and over.

"What are you doing?" Augustine asked.

"I'm going to empty the sea into the hole I dug in the sand," the child responded. "That's impossible," Augustine advised. "You'll never be able to fit the sea into that little hole."

The child looked up at the bishop: "And you will never be able to contain the infinity of God within the confines of your mind."

Those innocent but challenging words to the saint are a reminder to every spiritual seeker. Our minds cannot grasp the infinite mystery of the Holy One. Our journey toward God is a continuing pilgrimage toward a horizon that recedes as we approach. However, it is not a journey without hope. Many faiths teach that we are made in God's image (Genesis 1:26–27), and that our minds and hearts are meant to seek the infinite. For many spiritual pilgrims, God is the destination; relationship with the Divine is human destiny. We delight in searching for God, like a child immersed in the pleasures of infinite sand and endless sea. Yet in this life we must keep moving along, with the immensity of water to one side and our theological excavations to the other, knowing that regarding comprehension of God we are but children playing on the beach.

This story of Augustine and the child prompts another analogy, one related to the purpose of this book. During his long life of seventy-six years, Augustine wrote by most counts 252 books, 396 sermons, and 298 letters—these are the extant texts. My task is to introduce you to this great Christian thinker and spiritual teacher. To that end, from among the tens of thousands of pages he wrote, I have chosen a small selection of passages that best convey his life, thought, and work. In that daunting task, I have felt like the child on the beach. Augustine's writings are like a great sea; the depth and breadth of his thoughts stretch out to many distant theological shores. Each selection from his writings is but a small scoop from a vast ocean of ideas that have influenced and shaped Christian theology and Western philosophy in many ways. I chose selections that hopefully make his thought accessible without compromising its complexity, or excising its nuance.

Augustine's friend and first biographer, Possidius, wrote that "[s]o many are the works he dictated and published, so many the sermons he preached in church and then wrote down and revised, ... that even a student would hardly have the energy to read and become acquainted with all of them" (Possidius, *The Life of Saint Augustine* XVIII.9). This little volume offers you small shells brimming with his words, in hopes that you yourself might wade deeper into his thought, and perhaps embark on a further exploration of his teachings.

Faith, Grace, God, and the World

These selections from Augustine's writings are presented in four parts that organize and reflect major themes in his theology. The first part is "The Journey of Faith." The image of journey or pilgrimage is one that runs through many of Augustine's writings. He understood religious faith as an ongoing quest for ever deeper understanding of a person's convictions and their implications for how to live. How might we reflect rationally on the nature of God and converse reasonably with each other about faith?

Part Two, "Through Sin to Grace," explores how we struggle with the moral decisions and ethical directions that guide our lives. This section explores Augustine's teachings about human sinfulness, free will, and the divine grace that he believed heals and saves us. We will examine Augustine's challenges to rivals such as the Manichean religious sect and the British monk Pelagius who had alternate explanations of such topics.

Part Three, "Intent Upon God," presents selections from Augustine's thoughts on God as Trinity, and how we may come to know something about the divine mystery through Christian faith in Jesus Christ and the Holy Spirit. This section also highlights the importance of love, friendship, and community in Augustine's theology and spirituality. As a pastor and bishop, Augustine celebrated the sacraments and led his community in prayer and worship. This section looks at his thoughts on church life, and explores the conflicts he had with Donatist Christians of North Africa who had a more severe and exclusive take on church membership.

Even though Augustine kept his gaze fixed upon God, he was very much a man involved in the moral, social, and political issues of his day. His journey of faith, while intent upon God, led through the changing, troubled, and turbulent time of late Roman antiquity. In Part Four, "While in the World," we look at his writings and preaching about war, peace, and justice, about the importance of creation and human sexuality, and about social responsibility and citizenship.

Each of these four parts presents selections from Augustine's writings, with annotations that will, I hope, help you better understand and critique Augustine's ideas and positions on these various topics. I chose these selections with several criteria in mind: I wanted to give you a way into Augustine's thought by presenting his most accessible writings on a particular topic—not an easy task, given that Augustine never insults his readers' intelligence and has quite a bit to say on topics he considers important. I also wanted to expose you to as many of Augustine's books, sermons, and letters as it is possible to do in a short anthology. This was a difficult goal given the sheer volume of his writings. Finally, I did not presume any prior knowledge of Augustine and his thought, so this text is very much an introduction, an invitation to discover more about this early North African bishop by pursuing other books and commentaries. There are suggestions for further readings and other sources in Suggestions for Further Study (pages 211–212).

We will follow Augustine's thoughts about the journey of faith, about our struggles with sin, and about the God whose saving grace guides us through the world to ultimate union with the Divine. My annotations are designed to help you engage with Augustine, to situate his texts in the context of when and why he wrote them. They explain theological words for readers who may not be familiar with such vocabulary, and point to the subtexts of meanings and suppositions that lie below the words. Implications or applications of Augustine's thought for our own day are also suggested.

I expect that as we walk along together with Augustine we will encounter a mischievous, imaginative child or two who will interrupt Augustine's words, my comments, or your thoughts with an arresting question. Such angelic visitations, like Augustine's fabled encounter on the beach, are promptings of grace calling us to deeper reflection, inviting us to move from mind to heart, ultimately to dwell in the deepest recesses of the soul. It is there, at the very fundaments of self, that Augustine's thought has its deepest resonance. I hope your friendly angel will take you there.

A Brief Overview of Augustine's Life

Who was this man whose influence on Christianity and on Western civilization has been so pervasive? How did he come to be a Christian, a bishop, and a theologian? Augustine's many writings emerged organically from the struggles of his life and the challenges of his pastoral role. His literary works are an expression of his passion to understand and communicate the deeper meanings of human experience—his own and others.

Aurelius Augustinus was born on November 13, 354, in the North African town of Thagaste, the present Souk Ahkras in Algeria, about forty-five miles south of the Mediterranean coast. His father, Patricius, whom Augustine describes as outstandingly generous but hot-tempered (*Confessions* IX.9.19), was one of the thousands of proud, yet financially careworn, gentry of Rome's African Province of Numidia. His mother's name, Monica (also spelled Monnica), suggests that she was a native Numidian, a descendant of the indigenous peoples closely related to the modern-day Berbers. Augustine had perhaps two sisters and at least one brother, Navigius.

When North Africa was the prosperous, pleasant, and secure home of Augustine's youth, it had been a province of the Roman Empire for almost five hundred years. Africa provided wheat, corn, and oil for the Roman world. Its citizens were proud of their important role in the economy and culture of Rome, even if their more urbane cousins across the sea in Italia might have considered these southern colonials curious in their rural accent and extreme in their religious passions.

We know much about Augustine's youth from the early chapters of his famous book *Confessions*. Doted on by his mother at home, he was bright and arrogant in school. He hated the quick hand and sharp cane of his teachers. Virgil's adventure stories of Roman heroes like Aeneas excited the young Augustine's imagination and stirred his feelings. Homer's tales of earlier Greek champions were less accessible because Augustine had such distaste for Greek grammar. Augustine strove hard to be accepted by his peers as he grew into his second decade, engaging in juvenile pranks, which provided him much thought for reflection and regret in his adult years.

After finishing his primary education in the local school of Thagaste, he went to the town of Maduras, eighteen miles to the south. He continued his studies there from about twelve to fifteen years of age. His parents could not afford more than that, however, and he had to endure a stormy sixteenth year at home until Patricius secured a patron, an influential family friend named Romanianus. In 371, Augustine left for the port city of Carthage, about one hundred and seventy-five miles east on the Gulf of Tunis. He admits that his motives for going on to higher education were mixed at best: "So I arrived at Carthage, where the din of scandalous love-affairs raged cauldron-like around me. I was not yet in love, but I was enamored with the idea of love. (*Confessions* III.1)." The classical education waiting for him there was a ticket out of the poor, back country life in Thagaste.

During his student years in Carthage (371–74), Augustine began living with a girlfriend who was to be his faithful companion for thirteen or so years. Augustine never tells us her name. Together they had a son, Adeodatus, while Augustine was still a student at Carthage. During this time, Augustine also became a "hearer" (novice) in the Manichean religious cult, and suffered the death of his father, Patricius. All of these changes and choices in his life made for a tumultuous "college" career in any century. Indeed, Monica was so upset by Augustine's decisions that she at first refused to let him (and one presumes his new girlfriend) into the house when they returned to Thagaste (*Confessions* III.11.19).

In *Confessions*, Augustine reports that during his second year at Carthage he fell in love with learning (III.4.7.8). He was inspired to pursue wisdom upon reading *Hortensius*, a now-lost work of the Roman senator and philosopher Cicero. This exhortation to philosophy changed Augustine's life and instilled in him a love of learning and a thirst for truth. From the vantage point of his later years, Augustine understood this to be the beginning of his search for truth, which led ultimately to his conversion to Christ.

The cult that Augustine joined, the Manichean sect, was a combination of Christian teaching and Persian dualism founded by the second-century Persian teacher Mani. Manicheans preached two ultimate principles of good and evil: the lighter, spiritual world was good, and the heavier, material world, evil. These two forces were in constant conflict, even and especially in human beings: the soul being good, but the body and its needs, evil. Augustine seemed to have found in this dualistic mysticism a compelling approach to the problem of evil—but only for a few brief years. Though he maintained social contact with them up to and during his year in Rome, Augustine admits that after meeting the Manichean teacher Faustus, when the latter came to Carthage in 382 or 383, he found the sect's intellectual base weak and flimsy. Later, as a bishop, Augustine spent significant time and energy refuting the Manicheans, whose influence in Europe lasted for several more centuries.

In 383, after teaching rhetoric in Carthage for seven years, Augustine left for Rome. The students there were said to be more dedicated and less disruptive. However, Roman students had the habit of not paying their bills. Augustine, who was struggling financially, was frustrated by the situation. His unhappy year in Rome was made more miserable by a serious illness and a growing disillusionment with the Manichean sect.

His talent for rhetoric and teaching was brought to the attention of Symmachus, the prefect of the city of Rome. Through contacts and connections secured by Symmachus, Augustine was offered the prestigious and lucrative position of speech writer for the emperor. This meant a move to the imperial capital, which by the fourth century was the northern Italian city of Milan. Augustine moved there in 384. He was soon joined by his companion and their son, as well as by his mother, brother, and assorted cousins and friends.

Several important currents in Augustine's life converged in Milan. In this cosmopolitan city, he was introduced to the thought of the Neoplatonists, and Augustine found this philosophical school very compelling. Plotinus (d. 270 CE) had retrieved, revived, and reframed Plato's philosophy. It appealed to Augustine's growing metaphysical hunger, and it challenged his intellect in ways that Manichean thought never had.

Another influential factor of his Milan experience was the Catholic bishop of the city, Ambrose. This distinguished gentleman of noble background was a powerful rhetorician as well as a student of Neoplatonism, and a convincing interpreter of sacred scripture. Even the critical and discerning Augustine admired and strove to emulate Ambrose. Augustine would go to the cathedral church where Ambrose preached in order to listen to and learn from his rhetorical style. Since Ambrose was speaking about the Christian faith, however, Augustine began to hear the bishop's content even as he studied his delivery.

Finally, during Augustine's time in Milan, he experienced an enervating episode of life weariness. He had been responsible for supporting a family and the friends who would visit and stay. His intellectual search, always infused with passion and restlessness, was beginning to wear on him. Monica, never happy with his female companion, finally prevailed upon Augustine to send her back to Africa. Both found the separation devastating. Monica then arranged a proper marriage for him, a marriage delayed, however, by the young age of his fiancée. This sent Augustine off on another sexual fling, since, he confesses, he could not remain celibate while waiting for marriage. Finally, the competitive, corrupt, and deceitful world of fourth-century Roman politics, especially fierce in the imperial court, drained his energies.

Conversion and New Beginnings

Augustine recounts that, amidst all this inner turmoil and outer stress, he experienced a call to "Pick up and read" (*Tolle lege*) the New Testament. There, in his garden in Milan, he picked up Paul's letter to the Romans and read the beginning of chapter 14: "Not in dissipation and drunkenness, nor in debauchery and lewdness, nor in arguing and jealousy; but put on the Lord Jesus Christ, and make no provisions for the flesh and the gratification of your desires." This conversion experience was the beginning of his life as a committed Christian. He decided to forgo marriage, and in September of 386, an exhausted but newly confident Augustine left his position in the imperial court and retired to a friend's villa in the foothills of the Alps, in the village of Cassisiacum. There, with son, mother, brother, and friends, he hoped to regain his mental and physical health. The following spring Augustine, his son, and his good friend Alypius were baptized during the Easter Vigil on April 24–25.

He soon made plans to return home to Africa. Augustine's party, traveling by ship, was delayed in the Roman port city of Ostia because the harbor was closed by a military blockade. During the summer of 387, in Ostia, Monica died and was buried, never reaching the shores of her native land.

Back in Africa by 388, Augustine set up a religious commune on the family land he inherited in Thagaste. He intended to live a simple life of prayer and study with like-minded intellectual Christians. During the first or second year of this community living, his son, Adeodatus, died. After the separation from Adeodatus's mother and the death of Monica, the loss of his son was the third great heartbreak in a few short years for the thirty-five-year-old Augustine.

In the winter of 391, Augustine visited the port city of Hippo Regius, about fifty miles northwest of Thagaste. He was interviewing a potential new member for his community and somehow the Christians of the city knew he was in town. On a Sunday morning while he was attending Eucharist in the cathedral, the congregation seized him and presented him to their bishop, Valerius, for ordination as a priest. The old bishop may have been somewhat complicit in this plot to secure a worthy episcopal successor. Valerius ordained Augustine to the priesthood on the spot.

The recent convert was reluctant to leave his quiet community life of prayer and study. Augustine asked Valerius for several months to prepare himself for this new challenge. Then in early spring of 391, he moved to Hippo and began assisting the old bishop, even preaching for Valerius, who was Greek by origin and whose Latin was heavily accented. Augustine asked Valerius for permission to gather a community around him in Hippo, as he had in Thagaste, and thus was born the first Christian urban monastery. When Valerius died in 395, Augustine became bishop of Hippo, a ministry he continued for the next thirty-five years.

Theological Controversies and Ideas

Bishop Augustine cared passionately for the people he was ordained to serve. He employed his famous rhetorical skills and literary gifts for the preaching of the Gospel. In his many letters, sermons, and books, he addressed difficult questions of Christian doctrine and discipline. He probed into problems of belief and behavior, always seeking to get to the heart of the matter, to know as best as one might the truth.

As a pastor, he dedicated his keen intellect to respond to the questions and concerns of his congregation and to the problems and issues of the wider church in North Africa. Of his two hundred and fifty-two books, only five were written before he became a priest. The great majority of his writings are pastoral, that is, composed or—in the case of his sermons—delivered to help his fellow Christians understand their faith and grow in their spirituality.

Three major religious controversies occupied his literary and rhetorical energies over his many years in the ministry. As a young priest and bishop, he struggled to quell the contention and violence generated in the schism between the Christian sect of the Donatists, the radical Christian purists of North Africa, and his own Catholic Church. He confronted questions about good and evil and the nature of the universe raised by the Manicheans, the sect he joined while he was a student at Carthage. And, he argued against what he considered to be a self-justifying faith that was being taught by the British monk Pelagius, whose teachings on divine grace and human effort were not up to Augustine's standards.

In order to prepare you for Augustine's own words, we will review each of these three controversies, which occupy so much space in Augustine's writings. Then we will study a short overview of original sin and predestination—two challenging ideas that emerge amidst Augustine's theological arguments. This review is not meant to be a comprehensive introduction to Augustine's theology. Rather, it sets the historical context of fourth- and fifth-century North African Christianity in which Augustine lived, preached, and wrote.

Augustine and the Donatists: What Makes for a "Pure" Church?

When Augustine was ordained a priest in 391, he very quickly had to face a problem that was tearing the North African church apart—the problem of the Donatists. The Donatists were not doctrinal heretics. They did not teach any basic Christian doctrine that was fundamentally different from the Catholics. Rather, they were a schismatic sect, that is, they were similar in teaching and practice to the Catholics, but separated themselves from the Catholics over the practice of rebaptism.

Named after Donatus, one of the African bishops ordained in protest against the leadership of lapsed clergy, Donatism is an example of sectarian religion. It emphasized and understood the church to be the community of the pure and sinless, living apart from and persecuted by the tainted and sinful world. It was religion by exclusion.

In the third and early fourth centuries, before the Emperor Constantine decreed religious toleration in 313, Christians in North Africa were badly persecuted as enemies of the Roman state. Some died as martyrs rather than deny their faith. Others, however, gave in to the fear of suffering and death and betrayed their belief, in particular by handing over their books of scripture to the Roman authorities. Hence, they were *traditores*, which in Latin means "those who handed over" the sacred books. A third group consisted of those who were not traitors, but who sought some kind of accommodation with the Roman state. After the period of persecution ended, some of the traitors returned to the church and even to their ordained ministerial positions as priests or bishops. They, along with those who had urged accommodation, were considered suspect by the many who had suffered and endured. The traitors and compromisers were considered unworthy of communion.

The question arose as to whether anyone baptized by these once traitorous priests or bishops should be rebaptized. After all, did not their sin compromise their ability to administer the sacrament? In addition, the Donatists argued that people baptized by anyone but members of the true and faithful church, namely their own, needed to be rebaptized.

The North African church split over this. The Catholics said no: baptism was a once and for all event. The power of baptismal grace came from God, not from the minister who baptized, no matter what that minister had done in the past. The Donatists, on the other hand, insisted on a "pure" church, unblemished by sin or compromise. Local churches and dioceses split over this issue, and the division grew deeper and more virulent during the second half of the fourth century. It was common for there to be two feuding churches in most towns, each with their own bishop: one Catholic and one Donatist. They were similar in every respect, except on this issue of rebaptism.

To a significant extent, this religious schism was rooted in social differences, as often happens. The Donatists were especially numerous and powerful outside the main urban areas, among the rural peasants and migrant workers. There was also the difference between indigenous African Christianity, claiming heroes such as the third-century bishop of Carthage Cyprian, who himself was martyred, and the "imported" Christianity that came from the European continent. The latter, in the view of the Donatists, was associated with Rome and imperial affairs. Because of the social distinctions, and the religious fervor that North Africans brought to their faith, the religious difference of opinion grew violent. Many Catholic laypeople and clergy were physically assaulted and even murdered by Donatists. A particularly violent group among the Donatists were the Circumcellions, who wandered the countryside in roving bands, terrorizing, maiming, and killing Catholics. Catholic bishops, including Augustine, appealed to the civil authorities to mobilize imperial soldiers to stop this violence against their people.

In an attempt to settle differences and bring the violence to an end, a conference of Catholic and Donatist bishops was convened in Carthage in June 411. Augustine played a leading role at this conference, and his arguments helped the Catholic side to convince the civil authorities of the legitimacy of their cause. The Donatists were ordered to cease and desist and to enter a process of reconciliation and assimilation into the Catholic

Church. Donatist bishops were to be treated fairly and to retain their episcopal rank and church property as far as possible.

Unfortunately, the majority of Donatists did not abide by the decision of the conference at Carthage, and the violence against Catholics escalated. Augustine tried to find ways to settle things peacefully. However, in the end, stymied by the worsening violence, Augustine argued that the state had the right to impose this ecclesiastical decision on the Donatists, even by force. Augustine always argued that people should be treated with a view to their ultimate spiritual and physical welfare, and he wanted the most lenient punitive measures to be taken against perpetrators of violence. Yet his legacy bears the burden of state-imposed enforcement of a church decision. Given the circumstances of the time, it can be argued that Augustine had little choice but to invoke the force of the government to protect his people.

Unlike the Donatists, Augustine never understood the church to be a community of sinless, pure souls. It was rather a mixture of many kinds of persons, all in need of forgiveness. Judgment is to be deferred until the end of time, allowing time for sinners to repent. Nor did he understand the world beyond the church to be evil. He states often in *City of God* and other writings that many good people live in the world, identified not by membership in the church, but by their fundamental goodness and love of God. Augustine's approach to religion is one of inclusion, openness, and hope.

Augustine and the Manicheans: Responsibility for Our Choices
Augustine spent a good deal of time focusing on how we make decisions. In Book VIII of *Confessions,* he employs his literary and rhetorical skills to tell the story of the biggest decision in his own life: to leave his position in the Roman Empire, be baptized, and devote himself to a life of community prayer and study as a celibate Christian. One of his main purposes in writing *Confessions* was to encourage his readers to reflect on their own lives in the light of faith. So he invites people to consider how *they* make

decisions, for the journey of faith is a series of choices we make through-out life.

One way of framing Augustine's thinking about decision making is to highlight two contrasting schools of thought on choice: the Manicheans and the Pelagians. On one extreme were the Manicheans, a religious sect combining Persian mysticism, Christian doctrine, and ascetical discipline. Outlawed by the Roman Empire, the sect caught Augustine's attention during his student years in Carthage. Manicheans believed in two oppo-site, equal, ultimate forces: God, who was light, good, and ethereal; and the demon, or *Hyle*, who was dark, evil, heavy, and material. These two forces have made constant war on each other ever since they were comingled in the physical universe. One battlefield of this cosmic conflict is the human being. We are both spirit and matter, so we are a conflicted combination of goodness and evil, which battle each other in the many aspects of our lives.

According to Manichean teachings, the choices we make are not active exercises of free will. Rather, they are skirmishes between good and evil. In these confrontations between good and evil that are fought in our minds and bodies, we are alternately prisoner, collateral damage, or freed hostage. But, whatever the circumstances, we are not responsi-ble for our behavior, or for what happens in our lives, according to Manichean teaching. The goal of a Manichean is to refrain as far as pos-sible from involvement in the material world and physical desires. Such asceticism, they believed, defeats the influence of matter and advances the victory of the spiritual.

Augustine, the young student in Carthage, found this exotic Persian sect attractive. It let him off the hook. Moral choices were not really his to make. Life decisions were not the result of the exercise of his free will. They were reports received from the battlefront where good and evil were fighting it out. We can imagine the twenty-year-old student in Carthage dismissing responsibility for his sexual trysts, political maneu-vering, and personal manipulation of others. All such behaviors were not the result of his choices. Rather, they were the tactics and strategies of light and darkness using his weak human nature in their cosmic clash.

In short, Manichean teaching basically denies the existence of free will. We are passive pawns in the ongoing drama of universal good and evil. As a bishop, Augustine later wrote books and preached sermons against the sect.

Augustine and the Pelagians: A Free But Wounded Will

Between 411 or 412 and his death in 430, Augustine waged the greatest theological debate of his life. He argued forcibly and at length in many books, sermons, and letters against a group of Christian theologians that came to be called the Pelagians.

The sect got its name from the monk Pelagius, who came down to Italy and the Mediterranean from Britain. He was known for his exemplary life and devotion to the Gospel. Pelagius moved among the elite class of Christians and clerics in Italy and the imperial court. There, in these social contexts, he preached a strict asceticism. He taught that God enlightens the mind by divine grace and reveals the way a Christian should behave. Once enlightened about the way to act, it is up to us to perform accordingly. We have it within our power to choose the right and the good. Discipline over the body by fasting and other ascetical practices, as well as a strict regimen of prayer, all strengthen our resolve and prepare our will to make the right choices that God has revealed to us.

Pelagius also taught that human nature was not corrupted by the sin of Adam and Eve. Rather, we can change our habits of sin if we apply ourselves, steel our wills, and do the right thing. And, by the way, infants do not have to be baptized since there is no residual guilt or weakness from original sin.

Various Christians brought Pelagius's ideas to Augustine and asked for his opinion. He replied swiftly and directly: We all stand in need of God's healing grace, which both enlightens our minds to know the good *and* strengthens our wills to do it. Knowing the right thing to do is only half the battle. We need God's help to do the right and the good. Our will is weak, wounded by the original sin of Adam and Eve, in dire need of divine grace so that we can choose the good. Certainly, this was Augustine's own experience as he recounts in *Confessions*. We may know the right and good thing, but we are often unable to move in that direction. God's grace helps our will to do the right and good thing by attracting us to it. Convinced that Pelagius was dead wrong, Augustine believed that Pelagian theology undermined the very notion of salvation inherent in the Gospels by denying the sinful nature of humanity and attributing good works to human effort alone.

Augustine never met Pelagius—although he may have seen him once or twice from a distance in Carthage. But he mounted a formidable theological challenge that ended up with Pelagius's teachings being condemned by church councils in Africa and Jerusalem, as well as by the bishop of Rome and the imperial government. It is worth noting that Pelagius had his defenders among Roman courtiers and clerics, and that Rome was sometimes put off by the fierceness of African Christianity. One pope initially found no objections to the theology of Pelagius and his associates, until Augustine kept pressing the issue.

After his excommunication in 419, Pelagius faded into obscurity among monasteries in the East. But Julian, the young bishop of Eclanum in Campania, Italy, soon took up the Pelagian standard and charged right back at Augustine with a series of books in which he attacks the old bishop of Hippo both theologically and personally.

Original Sin: Defining Wounded Humanity and Its Salve

Original sin is one of Augustine's most famous and influential teachings, and one that we will review to help you approach Augustine's writings. He did not originate the idea, but he did coin the term, which in Latin is *peccatum originale*. It appears for the first time in 396, in Augustine's *Response to Simplician*. As recounted in Genesis 2 and 3, Adam and Eve lived in harmony with God and nature in the Garden of Eden. All things were theirs, except to eat fruit from the tree of the knowledge of good and evil in the middle of the garden. Scripture scholars tell us that "knowledge of good and evil" is an ancient poetic expression for the knowledge of all things, or omniscience. Since only God is omniscient, the sin of Adam and Eve was one of pride. They thought that the fruit of the tree of knowledge of good and evil would make them like God. In that desire and the act that followed, they betrayed the truth of their created nature.

Theologians prior to Augustine taught that all the descendants of Adam and Eve suffer effects from the sin of the first parents, though various writers explained those effects in different ways. Augustine's explanation of the effects of original sin came to dominate Christian thinking about the wounded nature of humanity and what seems to be our propensity, generation after generation, to perpetrate evil upon one another and upon the world.

According to Augustine, we inherit original sin by virtue of our being physical descendants of Adam and Eve. He calls original sin a kind of "infection" passed on through the man's semen. Original sin leaves our mind clouded and confused about what is good and right, and it leaves our will wounded and weakened when it comes to doing what is good and right. What's more, taught Augustine, we carry the guilt of Adam and Eve in our souls. That's why Christians baptize their infants: to remove the guilt of original sin, and to allow God's grace to begin to enlighten the mind and strengthen the will as the child grows.

In addition to the effects of Adam and Eve's original sin, which predispose us from birth to commit our own personal sins, Augustine believed there is also the effect of observation and habit. We are born into a world of sinners who have created an environment filled with evil deeds. As we grow and develop through childhood and adolescence, we imitate and repeat what we witness, spreading the virus of sin. Living in such a world, we quickly form habits of sin in our own lives that reinforce the effects of original sin. In Augustine's opinion, the human race is in a dire situation and stands in sorry need of rescue from the power of sin. As we shall see, he believed that it is only by God's grace that we are redeemed from this situation.

Over the centuries, many have considered Augustine overly pessimistic about human nature. In his own day, the Pelagians challenged Augustine's understanding of original sin and its consequences. They thought that his theology negated free will altogether. At times, his theology of original sin seems a heavy theological burden indeed. Certainly, Augustine cannot be accused of being Pollyannaish, nor of ignoring the persistence of inhuman, destructive behaviors propagated by so many. Yet, as we shall see, his theology of original sin is balanced by his theology of grace. Augustine's teachings on grace promote an understanding of redeemed and renewed humanity that invites human beings to friendship with God.

Predestination: God's Election of the Chosen

In the later years of his dispute with the Pelagians, especially in the books and letters he wrote against Julian of Eclanum, Augustine forged ahead boldly into a theological cul-de-sac where others were reluctant to follow. This was his teaching about predestination, which he drew from his interpretation of certain New Testament passages. This idea has periodically resurfaced in the history of Christian theology and practice.

Predestination is the belief that God has already decided, for all eternity, who will receive divine grace. Augustine was so adamant about exposing the Pelagian approach to grace for what he believed it was—a denial of salvation through Christ—that he fashioned and wielded this theological mace of predestination, which he swung hard and often in his final years.

The teaching of predestination is based on several scriptural passages:

> In love he destined us for adoption to himself through Jesus Christ in accord with the favor of his will, in him we were also chosen, destined in accord with the purpose of the One who accomplishes all things according to the intention of his will....
>
> —Ephesians 1:5, 11

He saved us and called us to a holy life, not according to our works but according to his own design and the grace bestowed on us in Christ Jesus before time began.

—2 Timothy 1:9

To sit at my right and at my left is not mine to give but is for those for whom it has been prepared by my Father.

—Matthew 20:23

Augustine used these texts to build once and for all what he considered to be an unassailable defense of his doctrine of divine grace against the likes of Julian. He thought that predestination, as detailed in scripture, proved that we are saved by God's grace alone, not by our own efforts at self-justification. Only grace can enlighten our minds and strengthen our wills. Whatever good we accomplish in this life, and however far we travel along the journey of faith, everything is due to God's love for us. In fact, Augustine claims, it has already been determined by God for all eternity those who will receive grace. These are the elect, God's chosen ones. The rest are the damned, the *massa damnata* or *massa perditionis*.

Augustine believed that salvation was only for those who were baptized in grace and who persevered to the end, aided by grace. All the nonbaptized, even infants and children, would go to hell (though Augustine allowed a hell of lesser pain—and he was troubled by his own theology on this point). All of this was preordained by God in the infinite, divine wisdom, which we should not presume to question or judge. With regard to salvation, Augustine thought that nothing is due to our efforts. Everything depends on God's grace.

We should remember that Augustine developed his ideas on predestination specifically in the heat of his argument with Julian and the Pelagians. Augustine particularly wanted to counter the self-assured ascetics who populated Pelagian communities. They stressed the importance of willpower in the spiritual struggle to perfect themselves. According to them, grace shows us the way, and then we forge ahead toward salvation on the strength of our prayer, fasting, and moral righteousness. Augustine's own experience, and the struggles of the common people for whom he was pastor, led him to a kinder, gentler theology in which God's love and forgiveness makes up for our persistent weakness. Predestination is his paradoxically extreme argument for the supremacy of love and grace.

Augustine is notably silent on the theme of universal salvation found in 1 Timothy 2:4: "God wills everyone to be saved and to come to knowledge of the truth." In fact, his teaching of predestination led to controversy during his life and ministry. Why then, should we even try to be good, if it is already decided? asked some African monks. How could he condemn innocent children to hell? asked Pelagius.

Augustine's theology of predestination, excessive by most theological standards, is balanced by other more moderate passages in his writings. Though he regularly insists on the sacrament of baptism as necessary for salvation, he also affirms in many places that before the coming of Christ, good people, especially the Hebrew prophets and prophetesses, received God's Holy Spirit (*Miscellany of Eighty-three Questions* LXII; *City of God* XVIII.47). Salvation was given to those innumerable generations who preceded the Hebrews of old, as well as to the Jews and non-Jews of antiquity, who by their piety and worship revered God (*Letter* 102.12; *On the Predestination of the Saints* 17.34). He even suggests that although hearing the preaching of the Gospel is indeed the ordinary way of salvation for Christians, this does not preclude the possibility that others are saved directly by God or through angels from heaven (*The Gift of Perseverance* 19.48). Such tolerance and openness to the presence and power of God in other religions and forms of worship, attested by a seminal Christian writer like Augustine, needs wider recognition today as we struggle to bridge the religious and cultural divides of our time.

After Augustine's death, most theologians and councils of the church shied away from his extreme interpretation of predestination. Though Christians understand baptism as the ordinary means of salvation, God's grace is not limited to the dispensation of ritual sacraments. The current *Catechism of the Catholic Church* advises that no one can say for sure who is or who is not saved. Best to leave such questions to God's love and providence (*Catechism of the Catholic Church* 847). If you survey the wider horizon of Augustine's writings, his many passages on God's love and on love itself as a divine reality break through the gloomy clouds of predestination that overshadowed his stormy controversy with Julian in the final years of his life.

Love, Hope, Belief: Augustine's Quest to Understand our Humanity

These three great theological controversies, against the Manicheans, the Donatists, and the Pelagians, shaped much of Augustine's writing. The themes of original sin, grace, and salvation run through the pages of his books, sermons, and letters as he toils to define basic Christian teachings. However, it would be a mistake—and it has been made more than once—to identify Augustine with his theological rhetoric and thereby limit our understanding of him to these dogmatic debates.

Augustine certainly was good at theological argument. He who once was the Roman emperor's orator had become a very eloquent spokesman for his church. It is also important to remember that religious and political leaders in antiquity were expected to argue forcibly and at length on behalf of the communities they represented. But to confine Augustine to doctrinal dispute is to miss the larger meaning of his life and thought. Beneath his theology and supporting it is his quest to understand what it means to be a human being in relationship with God, what it means to be able to reflect upon the possibility of relationship with God. Augustine's thinking goes beyond iterations of church dogma and discipline. His thought is rooted in his persistent questioning about what it means to be a human being who loves, hopes, and believes. This premise, that the best way into Augustine's writing is to scrutinize his anthropology—his understanding of human nature, of who and why we are—has shaped my selection of texts and my annotations on those texts. His theology is best understood and interpreted in the wider context of his own passionate, loving humanity.

Writings

The three great books that Augustine bequeathed to subsequent generations are *Confessions* (completed around 400), *The Trinity* (begun around 400 and completed in 419), and *City of God* (begun around 413 and completed in 426). They are undisputed classics in Christian and world religious literature. In these texts, Augustine again and again raises the centrality of God's freely given love and forgiveness, the universal presence and power of Christ, the importance of the scriptures in Christian life and learning, and reliance on God and God's grace as opposed to our own devices and human institutions.

Confessions

Augustine began writing *Confessions* around 397 at the age of forty-three. He had already been a Christian for ten years, a priest for six, and a bishop for two. Many Christians in North Africa and around the Mediterranean were curious about this once influential member of the Roman imperial court who had abandoned his promising political career only to resurface as leader of the Catholic Church in Hippo. Others remained concerned about the aggressive proselytizing he had done on behalf of the Manichean sect as the sect was still active in North Africa. There were also fellow believers who wanted to know more about his journey of faith. So Augustine wrote the thirteen books of his *Confessions* (each book would be chapter length by contemporary standards). With burning honesty, he revealed his inner life in a way no one had ever done before in Greek or Roman literature.

In the first nine books of *Confessions,* Augustine reflects on his childhood, adolescence, and young adult life up to the death of Monica in Ostia. It is not an autobiography in the modern sense of the term, but was more autobiographical than anything written earlier in Greek or Latin literature. With keen psychological insight, he probes into human motivation and weakness, especially his own. He reflects on selected events from his life in light of the Christian faith that guides his life now that he is a bishop and pastor. Throughout these nine books, Augustine introduces various theological themes, such as original sin, divine grace, concupiscence, free will—themes that fill his sermons, letters, and other books as well. Augustine alternates from narrating memories of his earlier days, to theological reflection inspired by those memories, to prayers of praise and thanks to God for being a hidden part of his young life guiding him on his search for truth. *Confessions* has been called "praying on paper."

Book X is a long reflection on the nature of memory and the five senses, and how they fit into the life of a Christian believer. It is characteristic of Augustine that, after recalling in the first nine books many memories from his early life, he composes an extensive reflection on the nature and use of memory itself. Much of Augustinian spirituality is drawn from Book X.

Books XI to XIII are long theological examinations of the meaning of Creation as recounted in the first chapter of the book of Genesis. Commentators over the centuries have wondered how these last three books fit into the more personal nature of the earlier books. The key to why *Confessions* ends with three books on Creation is to understand how important a proper appreciation of the goodness of Creation was for Augustine. Augustine's struggles with the Manichean sect as a young man impelled him as a priest and bishop to many years of reflection on the goodness of the created universe. Not long after his conversion and baptism, he attempted to write *On Genesis: A Refutation of the Manichees* (388–89). As a priest he penned *Unfinished Literal Commentary on Genesis* (393–95). Neither of these met his high standards, so he continued exploring what scripture teaches and what he believed about Creation.

In the late 390s, he finished *Confessions* with three books that combine scriptural exegesis or interpretation with long, prayerful meditations on the seven days of Creation as recounted in Genesis 1. A year or two later, he began his longest, most thorough work on the subject, entitled *The Literal Meaning of Genesis* (401–19). In short, the last three books of *Confessions* are both part of Augustine's continuing study of the Genesis narrative, as well as a way of understanding his own life in the wider context of God's ongoing process of creation.

Confessions remains a spiritual classic, translated into all of the world's major languages. It is among Augustine's most accessible writings and for the student of classical studies represents some of the most poetic prose of late Latin literature. As an elderly bishop looking back over his life and writings, he remarks that

> [t]he thirteen books of my *Confessions* praise the just and good God for my evil and good deeds and lift up human understanding and affection to God. At least, as far as I am concerned, they had this effect on me while I was writing them, and they have the same when I am reading them. What others think about them pertains to them. Yet, I know that they please and continue to please many people.
>
> —*Reconsiderations* II.6.32

The Trinity

Comprised of fifteen books (again, a book, or *liber*, is the equivalent of the modern-day chapter), *The Trinity* is certainly among the most difficult of Augustine's writings. Even he worried that it was so complex as to benefit only a few readers (*Letter* 169). Indeed, few readers can venture into this text without some sort of theological guide.

A guidebook would need to mention the major parts of the journey through this text. In Book I, he explains the Christian belief that the One God is three persons and that this faith is based on the testimony of the sacred scriptures. In Books II to IV, he reviews the many stories and testimonies in the Hebrew Bible (what Christians call the Old Testament) and New Testament where these three divine persons can be discerned in the varied instances of God's approach to humanity through the patriarchs, Moses, the angels, the prophets, and Jesus. He also highlights the Hebrew themes of the Word of God and the Wisdom of God as theological precursors to Christian belief in the Word and Spirit. Augustine is clear about his assumptions. His theology of the Trinity is founded in the scriptural texts that are the authority to which he assents in faith.

In Books V through VII, he reviews theological language that other theologians—from both the Latin- and Greek-speaking churches—have used in their writings about the Trinity, words such as "person" and "substance." Augustine notes both their usefulness and limitations. He outlines various rational, philosophical arguments, and explores linguistic and logical complexities involved in any attempt to reflect on the nature of God.

Augustine introduces his original theology of the Trinity in Book VIII. He suggests that we can see traces of the triune God in various triadic structures in the created world, especially in our experience as human beings, since we are made in God's image. Then from Book IX through Book XV, he elaborates on many different triads in human experience, which he claims reflect the triune nature of the Divine Artisan who created us. There is the trinity of the lover, the beloved, and the love they share between them (*The Trinity* VIII.5.14); the trinity of being, knowing, and loving that grounds our very experience (see also *Confessions* XIII.11.12); and the related trinity of mind, knowledge, and love. These and many other examples he cites provide analogies from our experience that suggest ways of meditating upon the triune nature of the One God who is the source that sustains all creation.

The analogy that Augustine claims best reflects the triune nature of God is the triad of memory, understanding, and will—distinct but interrelated human capacities that support and penetrate one another in mysterious fashion. And it is when we remember, seek to understand, and choose to love God that this threefold nature of the human mind or soul best reveals the Trinitarian nature of the One who created us. Selections from *The Trinity* presented in Part Three of this book will help the reader explore these profound theological ideas.

For almost twenty years, his pastoral duties and travels interrupted Augustine's work on this demanding text. As he returned again and again to the writing, Augustine assiduously reworked and edited his thoughts. At one point, a draft version of the first twelve books was stolen (so anxious were his "fans" to read them). This upset Augustine, as it would any careful author, and he complained that it made his subsequent editorial work more difficult. Finally, in 419 he sent a finished copy to Bishop Aurelius of Carthage, permitting all fifteen books to be "heard, read, and copied" (*Letter* 174), though he continued for several years to make explanatory additions to the text.

City of God

Augustine lived at a time of political upheaval, especially during his years as bishop. On August 24, 410 CE, at the head of an army of Visigoth soldiers, Alaric invaded the city of Rome. It was an event that sent shock waves throughout the empire. Rome had been the center of its empire since the first century BCE, and of a republic since the sixth century BCE—over nine hundred years of continuous Roman history. As the city was occupied and the empire threatened, political refugees crossed the sea to North Africa for safe havens like Carthage and Hippo.

Augustine's response to this catastrophe was both pastoral and intellectual: he received refugees into his diocese and also reflected on the meaning of this significant historical, political shift in light of his Christian faith. We find the beginning of these thoughts in a letter written in 411 or 412 to Marcellinus, a Christian who was imperial commissioner in Africa and Augustine's friend (*Letter* 138). In this letter, Augustine begins to outline ideas about Christianity and the state, ideas that eventually find their way into his longest single work, *City of God*.

This tome, which Augustine himself called a *magnum opus et arduum*—a long and difficult work—was written over fourteen years, from 412 to 426. It expounds Augustine's political theology and reprises many of his other theological reflections on themes such as faith, reason, sin, grace, will, Creation, the church, and scripture. It is as challenging a book to read as it was for Augustine to write. He presents exhaustive critical analyses of Roman history and historians, ancient philosophers and their theories, pagan religions and practices, and scriptural stories and their patriarchs and heroes. He demonstrates his vast knowledge of ancient history and philosophy, as well as his thorough examination of the Bible. Augustine is unabashedly Christian in his theory of history: the apex of history is the Christ event, when God entered human history to reveal its final goal. The meaning and goal of history is beyond history in the final union of all creation with its Creator.

The main thesis is summed up in a famous line from Book XIV: "Two loves built two cities: the earthly city created by love of self, carried to the point of contempt for God; and the Heavenly City, created by love of God, carried to the point of contempt for self" (XIV.28). Human will, then, is the determinant of human history—not the Greek idea of fate nor the supposed powers of multiple gods and goddesses. It is who and what human beings choose to love that matters.

According to Augustine, human will, as we have seen earlier, is weakened by original sin. So it is only by God's grace that human beings are able to know and choose the good. These choices move them through the ages of this world toward their final end of heaven, the fully realized City of God, symbolized in the Bible by Jerusalem, the city of peace. Those who refuse to cooperate with God's grace act in self-centered ways that ignore or oppose God. They build up the City of Man, symbolized by ancient Babylon. In Augustine's view, the fall of Rome was due to the injustice and moral corruption of its citizens, not to the spread of Christianity.

Augustine makes it clear that the church is not the same as the City of God. There are many in the church who do not make good choices and thereby contribute to the confusion and dissension that characterizes Babylon. Nor are political and social institutions beyond the church to be identified as the City of Man, for many who are not Christians are moved by grace to make good choices that build up the City of God. "The two cities are intertwined and mingled with each other in this world, until the Last Judgment separates them" (*City of God* I.35). In this world, the two cities are mixed in together, differentiated only by the character and quality of human decisions.

Other Writings

There are well over two hundred books that Augustine wrote on a great variety of religious and theological topics. Among his other influential books are the several volumes of *Commentaries on the Psalms,* in which he provides multilayered interpretations of the one hundred and fifty psalms in the Hebrew Bible, and his *Homilies on the Gospel of John* and *Homilies on the First Epistle of John*. These works reveal the depth of Augustine's spiritual and prayer life, as well as his pastoral dedication to the people he served as priest and bishop. Almost four hundred sermons and three hundred letters to friends and colleagues, some of great length, have also come down to us over the centuries and provide insights into the man behind the theology. I have drawn from as many of Augustine's writings as possible that were suitable for an introductory anthology such as this.

Augustine's Legacy

Augustine died on August 28, 430, in his beloved Hippo Regius. During his final illness, the city was under siege by the Vandal tribes that were sweeping across North Africa, after crossing over from the Iberian Peninsula. This invasion was a further blow to the ever-weakening Roman Empire. Catholic Christianity died in North Africa shortly after Augustine, since the invading Vandals were Arians who practiced Christian rituals but who did not accept the divine nature of Jesus. Two centuries later, Islam swept across the northern coast of the continent, pushing back the Arian tide and claiming the land for Allah. Christianity only returned to this part of Mediterranean Africa fifteen hundred years later with nineteenth-century French colonists.

To the good fortune of posterity, Augustine's library was saved by his fellow monks and clerics, as noted by his friend and first biographer,

Possidius. During Augustine's lifetime, many of his works were copied and circulated to churches, monasteries, and individuals around the Mediterranean. Nonetheless, the survival of his library in Hippo was both a remarkable and important feat. It may likely have been transported, along with his remains, to the Island of Sardinia sometime in the decades following his death.

It is difficult to underestimate Augustine's influence on the subsequent development of Christian thought and practice. His writings remained the theological norm in the Western Church from the fifth to the thirteenth century. With the rise of the European universities in the twelfth and thirteenth centuries, a new generation of Catholic theologians, such as Thomas Aquinas, continued to use Augustine's writings as the foundation upon which they built their own new understandings and explanations of Christian faith. At the beginning of the Protestant Reformation in the sixteenth century, a German Augustinian monk by the name of Martin Luther shaped the contours of reform theology using Augustine's basic theological tools of sin and grace. Thus, Augustine has been called the greatest Catholic and the greatest Protestant theologian.

The middle of the twentieth century saw a renewed interest in Augustine's thought. New methods of historical criticism and textual interpretation, first applied to biblical texts, were soon employed to gain a better appreciation of Augustine's writings in light of the issues of his own time, culture, and concerns. The boldness of Augustine's thinking about Christian faith broke through the crusty layers of medieval interpretations and Reformation politics that had obscured much of the dynamism of his own thought. New biographies that drew on the advantages of contemporary historical method shed new light on late Roman culture of North Africa in ways that make Augustine come alive for the contemporary reader.

All of this renewed scholarly interest in Augustine had an effect on the Catholic Church. At the Second Vatican Council in Rome, Augustine's thought was in many ways rediscovered by the church. The church's understanding of itself as the pilgrim people of God, its deeper appreciation of the sacraments and of sacred scripture, as well as a new openness to the world—these and other ideas emerged into the documents of Vatican II to some extent because of Augustine. He is the most quoted ancient father of the church in the documents of Vatican II. The dynamic nature of his thought, and the controversies which shaped it, have provided a new impetus for theological creativity and dialogue in the contemporary church—Protestant and Catholic. Augustine and Augustinian theology and philosophy continue to be the subject of thousands of books and articles by scholars from many Christian denominations and academic disciplines. There are as well innumerable websites devoted to Augustine.

A recurring phrase in Augustine's writing is the simple Latin expression *in Deum*. A philosopher colleague of mine once asked why Augustine did not use the more familiar (and he implied more correct) Latin phrase *in Deo,* which means "in God." *In Deum* has a very specific theological meaning for Augustine. He used it to mean "on the way to God," or "intent upon God." Augustine encouraged his fellow believers to "be one mind and heart intent upon God"—*cor unum et amina una in Deum* (*Monastic Rule* I.3). He believed that Christian faith—and, we might add, all vibrant, healthy religious faith—is a pilgrimage of the mind seeking to know God and a journey of the heart striving to love God. In this life, we are always on that journey, never arriving.

This anthology is best understood and used in Augustine's sense of "on the way." At its conclusion, you will hopefully have a better appreciation of Augustine. But you will have only begun. Ideally, this text will encourage you to proceed further down the road to ever wider vistas of the powerful thought of this son of North Africa. His own advice to you might be found in the following words he once addressed to his congregation: "Always add some more, always keep on walking, always forge ahead" (*Sermon* 169.18).

Now to Augustine's own words.

A Note on the Translation ☐

The majority of English translations of Saint Augustine's texts in this volume are from *The Works of Saint Augustine: A Translation for the 21st Century* and *The Augustine Series*, copyrighted by the Augustinian Heritage Institute, Villanova, Pennsylvania, and published by New City Press, Hyde Park, New York. This translation project is still in process and due to be completed by 2020. For more information, visit www.augustinian heritage.org

All selections from *City of God* are my translations, since this volume is not yet published in the Augustinian Heritage project. The following passages are also my translations: from *Instructing Beginners in the Faith* 12.17 and *Letter* 130.2.4.

Part One:
The Journey
of Faith

1 Throughout *Confessions,* Augustine makes constant allusions to scripture—both Hebrew scripture (Old Testament) and the Christian New Testament. In this first sentence, he snatches phrases from Psalms 47, 95, 114, and 146 and uses them to express his own praise of God. Augustine invites us to join him in prayer.

2 Augustine is referring specifically to the Christian New Testament. "Carry our mortality about with us" is from Saint Paul's Second Letter to the Corinthians 4:10. "You thwart the proud" is from Peter's First Letter 5:5. After his conversion and baptism, the Bible became the focus of Augustine's faith and the guide for his prayer. *Confessions* is a primer in bringing scripture alive by relating it to and integrating it with one's lived experience.

It is helpful to remember that most people in his own day, and for centuries after, would have encountered *Confessions* by listening to someone read it aloud, since literacy was a privilege of the few.

3 This last phrase is among the most quoted from all of Augustine's works. Other translations read "our heart is restless until it rests in you." For Augustine, the life of faith is a constant search and continuing journey on the way to God.

➤ *Confessions,* Augustine's personal narrative, is essentially a long prayer to God. We listen in as Augustine praises God, wrestles with his own sinfulness, explores philosophical ideas in God's hearing, and remembers poignant events from his life up to and including the death of his mother in 387. All this literary effort is a labor of love and faith: love for God—"You pierced my heart with your Word, and I fell in love with you" (*Confessions* X.6.8)—and faith in God—"that faith which you have kindled, lamp-like, on my nocturnal path" (*Confessions* XIII.14.15). For sixteen hundred years, this work has fascinated readers of many religious and philosophical persuasions with its introspection, honesty, and openness. Augustine interweaves faith and doubt, prayer and philosophy, experience and reflection in ways no one ever had.

☐ Unquiet Hearts

Great are you, O Lord, and exceedingly worthy of praise; your power is immense, and your wisdom beyond reckoning.[1] And so we humans, who are a due part of your creation, long to praise you—we who carry our mortality about with us, carry the evidence of our sin and with it the proof that you thwart the proud.[2] Yet these humans, due part of your creation as they are, still do long to praise you. You arouse us so that praising you may bring us joy, because you have made us and drawn us to yourself, and our heart is unquiet until it rests in you.[3]

CONFESSIONS I.1.1

1 Take note of the short, direct sentences. How different they sound from the long, literary phraseology in *Confessions* and in the other books Augustine wrote. This is the more personal, more informal pastor speaking directly to his people. We know that he prepared to preach by meditating on and praying over the scriptural passage of the day's liturgy. He did not write a text from which he read, but rather, like other public speakers in antiquity, spoke extemporaneously. Stenographers copied his words as he preached.

2 The "someone there" is God. The divine indwelling is a constant theme in Augustine's preaching and writing. In Book III of *Confessions*, he writes that God is "more intimately present to me than my innermost being" (III.6.11).

3 Humility is a favorite theme of Augustine. By humility Augustine did not mean self-abasement and self-effacement. He meant the constant struggle to be as self-aware and as self-honest as possible. Humility is truth. It's a neverending task, as he stresses in this sermon.

🪝 Augustine delivered this sermon during a visit to Carthage in 416, almost twenty years after he had written *Confessions*. He was preaching on a passage from Saint Paul (Philippians 3:3–16), exhorting to his fellow Christians to reflect on the progress of their own spiritual journeys, as he himself had done in *Confessions*.

He encouraged them to be as honest with themselves as possible about their behavior, about their motivations, and about their feelings, and to commit themselves to continuous growth in faith and love. Honest self-evaluation is the way of the spiritual pilgrim. Clear-sighted introspection is the path toward God who constantly calls out to us from the future. So the life of a Christian, indeed of any spiritual seeker, is a constant pilgrimage on the way to God. As he writes in his commentary on Psalm 61: "Everything for us is pilgrimage" (*Expositions of the Psalms* 61.7).

☐ Keep On Moving

Forge ahead, my brothers and sisters; always examine yourselves without self-deception, without flattery, without buttering yourselves up.[1] After all, there's nobody inside you before whom you need feel ashamed, or whom you need to impress. There is someone there,[2] but one who is pleased with humility; let him test you.[3] And you, too, test yourself. Always be dissatisfied with what you are, if you want to arrive at what you are not yet. Because wherever you are satisfied with yourself, there you have stuck. If, though, you say, "That's enough, that's the lot," then you've even perished. Always add some more, always keep on walking, always forge ahead. Don't stop on the road, don't turn round and go back, don't wander off the road.

SERMON 169.18

1 Note the theme of proceeding, of walking with the writer, which is part of Augustine's Introduction to this book. He asks us to agree, disagree, and challenge him as we accompany him along the way of this treatise. For Augustine, the spiritual pilgrimage is not casual travel; the journey of faith is not aimless wandering. It is an intentional quest to which one brings not only the passion of faith, but also the resources of reason, the intensity of questioning, and the benefit of argument.

2 Here Augustine asks spiritual pilgrims both to challenge and to support each other in love as they travel through life. He counsels those who make the journey of faith to take an interest in each other's struggles along the way and to delight in the insights they share. We should not engage in theological argument for argument's sake. Rather, faith is a day-to-day struggle and a constant search for truth on the way to our goal, which is God (*Confessions* X.23.33).

3 We embark together on the pilgrimage of faith with other spiritual seekers, engaging our differences as a way of moving forward. Augustine names this compact among those who share the journey of faith a "covenant"—reminiscent of God's own covenant of love with us.

That covenant of love and faith is recalled by Christians in their celebration of the Eucharist and other sacraments. God's covenant community is also at the heart of the weekly Jewish Sabbath and annual feasts such as Passover, which recalls the birth of the covenant community and the beginning of the Hebrews' journey of faith through the desert toward the Promised Land.

□ Searching Minds

Accordingly, dear reader, whenever you are as certain about something as I am go forward with me; whenever you stick equally fast seek with me; whenever you notice that you have gone wrong come back to me; or that I have, call me back to you.[1] In this way let us set out along Charity Street together, making for him of whom it is said, *Seek his face always* (Psalm 105:4).[2] This covenant, both prudent and pious, I would wish to enter into in the sight of the Lord our God with all who read what I write, and with respect to all my writings....[3]

THE TRINITY I.1.5

1 For Augustine, there are two ways of knowing: one is the way of faith or belief, and the other is the way of reason or understanding. They are both valid, both necessary for the journey of faith, like food and drink for the spiritual pilgrim's sustenance.

2 Augustine spent a good deal of time and spilled a great deal of ink on the nature of faith or belief as a way of knowing. Faith is an act of the will, a decision to accept information or knowledge received from someone else. Faith is a rational act because it involves reflecting carefully on what we hear or receive from another before we accept it. We strive to validate thoughtfully what is reported to us by whatever authority we judge trustworthy. Augustine's definition of faith as "thinking with assent" can enrich theological reflection in other religious traditions as well.

We can think without believing, as for example when we consider what is right in front of us perceived directly through our senses, or when we reflect on the constant truth of a mathematical formula. But we cannot believe—we should not believe—without thinking carefully about what it is that we have decided to accept on the testimony of another. Every act of faith, as Augustine puts it so succinctly, is a "belief in thinking" itself. Religious sentiment or opinion, devoid of any probing reflection and thoughtful critique, does not rise to the level of what Augustine meant by faith.

☐ Faith Seeking Understanding

Understand, in order to believe; believe, in order to understand.[1]

SERMON 43.9

The very act of believing is nothing other than to think with assent. Not everyone, after all, who thinks believes, for many think in order not to believe. But everyone who believes thinks, and a believer thinks when believing and, in thinking, believes.... For, without thinking, there is no faith at all....[2]

ON THE PREDESTINATION OF THE SAINTS 2.5

3 Augustine presents the pervasiveness of belief in ordinary life. If we waited for immediate perceived validation of everything, the ambit of our lives would shrink considerably. Even the most stringent scientist whose method adheres strictly to experimental observation and controlled repetition resorts to belief upon leaving the laboratory to negotiate daily life. And the scientific method itself is thoughtful testing of information and conclusions received from other scientists, which requires a belief in the validity of their scientific assumptions and methods.

So the religious believer or spiritual seeker receives testimony and wisdom from others about ultimate questions. The responsibility of faith requires that we reflect thoughtfully and exercise our reason carefully concerning the religious teachings we receive and choose to accept as our own. Faith is an adult activity, but we are not alone in trying to discern what to believe. For Augustine, the divine light dwells in our minds, guiding us along our search for truth: "It is you, Lord, who will light my lamp: O God, you will illuminate my darkness...." (*Confessions* IV.15.25).

Far be it from us either to deny that we know what we have learnt on the testimony of others; otherwise we would not know the Ocean exists; we would not know that there are countries and cities commended to us by their celebrity and renown; we would not know that the men and their works, which we have learnt about from our historical reading, really existed; we would not know the things that are reported to us every day from all sides, which are confirmed by constant and consistent indications; finally we would not know where we were born or of what parents, because these are all things that we have believed on the testimony of others.[3]

THE TRINITY XV.4.21

✎ Augustine's faith journey led him through a time of profound doubt. This occurred during his year of teaching in Rome, and in Milan before he met the Neoplatonist Christians there. The Greek philosophical school known as the skeptics of the New Academy taught that no truth could be known for certain. So they counseled continued questioning and constant searching that never arrived at the destination of truth.

While he took this approach for a short while before his conversion, Augustine ultimately rejects skepticism. He affirms our capacity to arrive at truth. However, as we have already seen, embracing truth through faith does not mean the end of our search. The journey of faith requires ongoing exploration of the truth in which we believe, and a constant search for its implications for our lives.

Augustine explores these ideas in *Contra Academicos* (*Argument with the Skeptics*), a book he wrote shortly after his conversion. In this work, he reviews various Greek philosophical schools of skepticism.

1 There can be times when we, as spiritual pilgrims, wander through dark valleys, wondering if we are heading in the right direction, even doubting that there is any right direction or ultimate goal. Such doubt and skepticism was part of Augustine's journey, as he tells us in *Confessions*.

2 Many years later, in *City of God*, Augustine reprises his argument against philosophical skepticism. Using his reason alone, Augustine establishes the reliability of *being* (I am), *knowing* (I know that I am), and *loving* (I love that I am and that I know I am). His Christian faith leads him to detect a trace of the Divine One in this trinity of assurance: *being* reflects God the Creator; *knowing*, God the Eternal Word and Wisdom; and, *loving*, God the Holy Spirit in all creation (see *The Trinity* XV.12–17).

3 Augustine anticipates Descartes' famous seventeenth-century philosophical assertion "I think, therefore I am" with his own fifth-century subversion of skepticism.

☐ Doubt and Skepticism

A suspicion had arisen in my mind that another class of philosophers, known as Academics, were more likely to be right. These men had recommended universal doubt, announcing that no part of the truth could be understood by the human mind.... Accordingly, I adopted what is popularly thought to be the academic position, doubting everything and wavering....[1]

CONFESSIONS V.10.19; V.14.25

I am completely certain that I exist, and that I know I exist, and that I love that I know this.[2]

CITY OF GOD XI.26

I am deceived, therefore I am.[3]

CITY OF GOD XI.26

◥ Despite doubts and uncertainty, the journey of faith at some point involves an act of faith, a decision of the will, a reasonable assent to some type of authority that provides the assumptions and principles that guide the rest of our lives. In Book VIII of *Confessions,* Augustine retells the story of his conversion, his decision of faith. It was a struggle that had been building to a climax over many years. Even in the final moments of this struggle, his will waivered, his assent dissembled. It is easy to claim in a philosophical treatise, as Augustine did, that "[t]he very act of believing is nothing other than to think with assent." It is quite another thing to move beyond skepticism and make that crucial act of faithful assent, as these dramatic paragraphs from *Confessions* testify.

1 This is characteristic of Augustine's quest for self-honesty. He challenges us to ask of ourselves how much of our lives is pretending. We can so easily fool ourselves about our motivations, as Augustine admits he was doing. He had made a habit of pretending.

2 The familiar image of the drowsy sleeper, reluctant to leave the cozy warmth of bed and begin the day, is a compelling analogy for the weakness of our will. Augustine put off his decision of faith for months, even after he was intellectually convinced about Christian faith. Why? Augustine did not want to give up his free-wheeling lifestyle. The thoughtful assent that faith involves has real-life consequences. His will was too weak to take the next step. As we shall see, in Augustine's theology, only God's grace empowers the will to make an act of faith.

☐ The Will to Believe

I had grown used to pretending that the only reason why I had not yet turned my back on the world to serve you was that my perception of the truth was uncertain, but that excuse was no longer available to me, for by now it was certain.[1] But I was still entangled by the earth and refused to enlist in your service, for the prospect of being freed from all these encumbrances frightened me as much as the encumbrances themselves ought to have done.

I was thus weighed down by the pleasant burden of the world in the way one commonly is by sleep, and the thoughts with which I attempted to meditate upon you were like the efforts of people who are trying to wake up, but are overpowered and immersed once more in slumberous deeps.... It often happens that a person puts off the moment when he must shake himself out of sleep because his limbs are heavy with a lassitude that pulls him toward the more attractive alternative, even though he is already trying to resist it and the hour for rising has come; in a similar way I was quite sure that surrendering myself to your love would be better than succumbing to my lust, but while the former course commended itself and was beginning to conquer, the latter charmed and chained me. I had no answer to give as you said to me, *Arise, sleeper, rise from the dead: Christ will enlighten you* (Ephesians 5:14), and plied me with evidence that you spoke truly; no, I was convinced by the truth and had no answer whatever except the sluggish, drowsy words, "Just a minute," "One more minute," "Let me have a little longer." But these "minutes" never diminished, and my "little longer" lasted inordinately long....[2]

CONFESSIONS VIII.5.11,12

15

1 Cicero was the great Roman philosopher and statesman who lived in the time of Julius Caesar. He translated many books of Greek philosophy into Latin, provided commentaries, and introduced philosophical thinking and language into Roman culture. As an eighteen-year-old student in Carthage, Augustine read this book of Cicero's, which awakened in him a desire to attain wisdom. The *Hortensius* was lost to posterity except for snatches of the text that appear in the works of Augustine and other ancient writers.

2 So adolescence was "miserable" even in the Roman Empire of the fourth century!

☐ Give Me Chastity–But Not Yet

I felt myself loathsome, remembering how many of my years—twelve, perhaps—had gone to waste, and I with them, since my nineteenth year when I was aroused to pursue wisdom by the reading of Cicero's *Hortensius*.[1] I had been putting off the moment when by spurning earthly happiness I would clear space in my life to search for wisdom; yet even to seek it, let alone find it, would have been more rewarding than discovery of treasure or possession of all this world's kingdoms, or having every bodily pleasure at my beck and call. I had been extremely miserable in adolescence, miserable from its very onset, and as I prayed to you for the gift of chastity I had even pleaded, "Grant me chastity and self-control, but please not yet."[2] I was afraid that you might hear me immediately and heal me forthwith of the morbid lust, which I was more anxious to satisfy than to snuff out.

3 Beyond the sexual allusions of Augustine's imagery, notice the reference to "habit." Habit can be the enemy of will when we seek to change long-established behaviors.

This passage moves us further into Augustine's conversion story in Book VIII of *Confessions*. He focuses on the relationship between will and sexuality. For Augustine, as for many ancient philosophers influenced by Plato, sexual desires are presented as the most difficult for us to control by sheer force of will. Certainly that was Augustine's experience—not that he was an incorrigible playboy. After a series of relationships during his first year of study in Carthage, he was faithful to his son's mother for the thirteen years they were together—and he was deeply in love with her. "So deeply was she engrafted into my heart that it was left torn and wounded and trailing blood," when they separated in 386 (*Confessions* VI.15.25).

But soon after she left, he quickly picked up another woman on the rebound, even while he was waiting for his ten- or twelve-year-old arranged fiancée to come to marriageable age. But the ideal of the celibate and chaste Christian philosopher, seeking wisdom in company with others, had captured Augustine's imagination. This ideal is not quite the *sine qua non* to us today as it was for Augustine in his time and place. And the contemporary reader might yearn to advise: "Don't you know you can love a woman and still be a good Christian seeking wisdom?"

Celibacy was not yet required of priests or bishops in the fourth and fifth centuries. But Augustine was not at all interested in the ministry. What he wanted was to devote his life to the pursuit of wisdom and truth, unfettered by the responsibilities of family and household, and undistracted by any one relationship. As far as he was concerned, his sexual drive had to be denied since it inevitably led back to such responsibilities and such a relationship.

Yet he could not get control of his desires. So in *Confessions*, he uses (one might even say abuses) human sexuality as the illustration *par excellence* of how wounded and helpless the human will actually is.

Was anything left unsaid in my inner debate? Was there any whip of sage advice I left unused to lash my soul into coming with me, as I tried to follow you? It fought and resisted, but could find no excuse. All its arguments had been used up and refuted, but there remained a dumb dread: frightful as death seemed the restraining of habit's oozy discharge, that very seepage which was rotting it to death.[3]

Confessions VIII.7.17, 18

⌐ So effective is Augustine's writing style that his pages on sex and lust can distract the reader from his commentary on pride, ambition, and lying. It was not only his sexual desires that hampered Augustine's will to believe. Augustine admits over and over in *Confessions* that he was an ambitious, prideful, and deceitful courtier of Milan, the capital city of the empire at that time, ready and willing to climb over anyone to garner riches, achieve success, and gain worldly power. This vignette about a drunken beggar powerfully captures these themes.

1 One thinks of the pervasive spin doctors in Washington, D.C., and other world capitals, of the subjective and selective slant in media reports, and of all other kinds of political and personal deception that ruin lives and destroy relationships. Augustine lied with the best of them in the empire, and probably bested many. Later, as a bishop, Augustine wrote three books on the topic of lying.

2 Note the phrases Augustine uses to describe his inner state at this time of his life when he was externally so successful and at the height of his career: a heart panting with anxiety; seething with feverish, corruptive thoughts; dragging a heavy load of unhappiness; full of foreboding; apprehensive, torn with cares. Sounds like the intake form at a clinic for overstressed executives! Augustine's position as *rhetor* to the emperor was one of the most prestigious in the empire—and one of the most nerve-wracking. Augustine's successor in that position eventually went on to become Roman emperor himself, until he was deposed shortly thereafter.

☐ The Will to Power

I recall how miserable I was, and how one day you brought me to a realization of my miserable state. I was preparing to deliver a eulogy upon the emperor in which I would tell plenty of lies with the object of winning favor with the well-informed by my lying; so my heart was panting with anxiety and seething with feverish, corruptive thoughts.[1] As I passed through a certain district in Milan, I noticed a poor beggar, drunk, as I believe, and making merry. I groaned and pointed out to the friends who were with me how many hardships our idiotic enterprises entailed. Goaded by greed, I was dragging my load of unhappiness along, and feeling it all the heavier for being dragged. Yet while all our efforts were directed solely to the attainment of unclouded joy, it appeared that this beggar had already beaten us to the goal, a goal that we would perhaps never reach ourselves. With the help of the few paltry coins he had collected by begging, this man was enjoying the temporary happiness for which I strove by so bitter, devious, and roundabout a contrivance. His joy was no true joy, to be sure, but what I was seeking in my ambition was a joy far more unreal; and he was undeniably happy while I was full of foreboding; he was carefree, I apprehensive.... He would sleep off his intoxication that same night, whereas I had slept with mine and risen up again, and would sleep and rise with it again ... how many days!... There was a vast distance between us: he was the happier, not only in as much as he was flooded with merriment while I was torn with cares, but also because he had earned his wine by wishing good day to passers-by, while I was seeking a swollen reputation by lying.[2]

CONFESSIONS VI.6.9, 10

⌐ Augustine has been called the philosopher of the will. No one in Greek or Roman philosophy before him had written so extensively on the will as a human faculty. For Augustine, the will is what ultimately defines our humanity, for love is an exercise of will, and love, love of God and each other, is the purpose for which we have been made. His *Confessions* are a long theological reflection on will and its weakness, and our need for God's healing help.

1 Alypius was Augustine's lifelong friend. He features prominently in *Confessions*, first as Augustine's student, then as his colleague and housemate. Friends were a very important part of Augustine's life, and they share in the deepest moments of his life. Alypius's presence at Augustine's conversion is an example of how the journey of faith is both solitary and shared.

2 As Augustine relates the dramatic details of his conversion experience, he reintroduces the themes of journey, travel, and movement. The place of his conversion is a garden—no doubt an intentional allusion to the scriptural gardens of Eden, of Gethsemane, and of the Risen Lord's tomb, which was in a garden (John 20:11–18). Augustine's inner journey of conversion leads to and through these archetypal gardens.

☐ The Divided Will

Adjacent to our lodgings was a small garden. We were free to make use of it as well as of the house, for our host, who owned the house, did not live there. The tumult in my breast had swept me away to this place, where no one would interfere with the blazing dispute I had engaged in with myself until it should be resolved.... So I went out into the garden, and Alypius followed at my heels; my privacy was not infringed by his presence, and, in any case, how could he abandon me in that state?[1] We sat down as far as possible from the house. I was groaning in spirit and shaken by violent anger because I could form no resolve to enter into a covenant with you, though in my bones I knew that this was what I ought to do, and everything in me lauded such a course to the skies. It was a journey not to be undertaken by ship or carriage or on foot, nor need it take me even that short distance I had walked from the house to the place where we were sitting; for to travel—and more, to reach journey's end—was nothing else but to want to go there, but to want it valiantly and with all my heart, not to whirl and toss this way and that, a will half crippled by the struggle, as part of it rose up to walk while part sank down....[2]

3   The theme of the divided will is an important part of Augustine's intellectual legacy in Western philosophy. Part of Augustine's agenda here is to refute the Manichean sect, which taught that our actions are not the result of our own will, but of the competing powers of good and evil that combat each other within and through us, "two natures, one good, the other evil, each with a mind of its own" (*Confessions* VIII.10.22). Augustine's conversion story frames his theological argument for the centrality of will. One's will can often be divided, but the division is within oneself and calls us to a resolution for which we ourselves are responsible, and for which only God's grace is sufficient.

The mind commands the body and is instantly obeyed; the mind commands itself and meets with resistance. When the mind orders the hand to move, so smooth is the compliance that command can scarcely be distinguished from execution; yet the mind is mind, while the hand is body. When the mind issues its command that the mind itself should will something (and the mind so commanded is no other than itself), it fails to do so. How did this bizarre situation arise, how develop? As I say, the mind commands itself to will something; it would not be giving the order if it did not want this thing; yet it does not do what it commands.

This partial willing and partial nonwilling is thus not so bizarre, but a sickness of the mind, which cannot rise with its whole self on the wings of truth because it is heavily burdened by habit. There are two wills, then, and neither is the whole: what one has the other lacks.[3]

CONFESSIONS VIII.8.19, 21

Part Two:
Through Sin
to Grace

✎ In his *Confessions,* Augustine devotes many passages to refuting the Manichean sect, which he had once aggressively promoted. As a Catholic bishop, he was embarrassed by his former association with Manicheans and concerned that his rejection of their doctrine be clear and unequivocal.

1 Mani (216–77), the founder of the Manicheans, lived in the Persian Empire and belonged to a Jewish Christian sect. He was familiar with both Christian doctrine and the ancient Persian teachings of Zoroaster, as well as with Buddhist thought (he had traveled to India). He developed a system of religious teaching and ritual that combined elements of Christianity with Persian dualism. As it spread west from Persia into the Roman Empire, its adherents considered themselves a purer form of the Christian religion. So, as Augustine mentions, they used Christian vocabulary. They also were fond of repeating religious sayings and philosophical formulae. Hence Augustine calls them "chatterboxes" and "exceedingly talkative" (perhaps like modern-day religious enthusiasts or cultists who want to enlist us in their movement).

2 Manichean cosmology distinguished between five caves of evil: darkness, smoke, evil wind, evil fire, and evil water; and five good elements: light, air, wind, fire, and water. Their liturgies included the reading of texts—many written by Mani himself—and elaborate rituals about which we know very little. Jewish rituals and the sacred texts of the Hebrew Bible were all considered to be part of the kingdom of darkness. Augustine in his many anti-Manichean texts, sermons, and letters rails against Manichean deprecation and rejection of Jewish writings.

3 The sect had two levels of membership: hearers and the elect. The elect were an elite group who led celibate lives and practiced a strict asceticism of prayer and fasting. They avoided contact with the physical world as much as possible, shunning the cultivation and preparation of food, as well as all sexual activity. The hearers—of which Augustine was one—would prepare food for the elect and attend to their other needs. As a hearer, Augustine participated to some extent in Manichean liturgy and accepted, as he mentions, their mythology.

☐ The Devil Made Me Do It

I fell among a set of proud madmen, exceedingly carnal and talkative people in whose mouths were diabolical snares and a sticky mess compounded by mixing the syllables of your name, and the names of the Lord Jesus Christ and the Holy Spirit, who is our Paraclete and Consoler.[1] These names were never far from their mouths, but amounted to no more than sound and the clacking of tongues, for their hearts were empty of the truth.

CONFESSIONS III.6.10.

The fables of schoolmasters and poets are far better than the snares then being set for me; yes, verses, songs, and tales of Medea in flight are undeniably more wholesome than myths about the five elements being metamorphosed to defeat the five caverns of darkness.[2] These latter have no truth in them at all and are lethal to anyone who believes them, whereas I can turn verse and song into a means of earning real food. When I sang of Medea in her flying chariot, I was not vouching for any of it as fact, nor, when I listened to someone else singing of it, did I believe the story; but I did believe the Manichean lies.[3] All the worse for me!

CONFESSIONS III.6.11.

4 In this and the following sentence, Augustine gives us a summary of his days in Carthage—both as a student and later as a teacher. On the surface he was an arrogant, successful academic who participated fully in all that Carthage had to offer. Secretly (since the Manichean sect was officially outlawed, though rarely prosecuted), he practiced Manichean rituals to cleanse himself of the impurities he incurred through his lifestyle. It was a cycle of sin and cleansing that did not require any real conversion or change—since the sexually active Augustine apparently had little or no intention of becoming a more observant, celibate member of the Manichean elect.

5 One of the practices of the Manichean elect was ritual eating. By consuming certain foods like fruit, the elect's digestive processes would "free" the good particles of light mixed in the food substance and then belch them out to rejoin the other particles of light. All physical creation was an unholy mixture of particles of light and darkness, and members of the elect participated in the emancipation of light from matter. This would eventually lead to their salvation in the kingdom of light. The rest of us would unfortunately go to the darkness of hell.

Throughout those nine years, from my nineteenth to my twenty-eighth year, I and others like me were seduced and seducers, deceived ourselves and deceivers of others amid a welter of desires: publicly through the arts reputed "liberal," and secretly under the false name of religion.[4] In the one we were arrogant, in the other superstitious, and in both futile; under the auspices of the former, we pursued trumpery, popular acclaim, theatrical plaudits, song competitions, and the context for ephemeral wreaths, we watched trashy shows and indulged our intemperate lusts; through the latter, we sought to be purged of these defilements by providing food for the so-called elect or saints, in the hope that they would turn the food into angels and gods for us in the workshops of their bellies to be the agents of our liberation.[5] These ends I pursued, these things I did, in the company of friends who through me and with me were alike deceived.

CONFESSIONS IV.1.1.

1 In the middle of Book III of *Confessions*, where he recounts and renounces his years with the Manicheans, Augustine inserts this reflection on various motivations for sinning. His point is that our evil tendencies and deeds are not the result of some cosmic darkness that is trapped in our flesh. They result from our wounded human nature and our weakened will—both results of original sin (an idea which we will consider shortly).

2 The "three plus seven" refers to the Ten Commandments or Decalogue. The first three commandments concern our relationship with God; the remaining seven, relationships with our neighbor.

☐ Our Sins Are Our Own

The Manicheans ... blaspheme ... by introducing two natures—a good one, which they call God, and another, an evil one, which God did not make.

THE NATURE OF THE GOOD 41

It is the same with crimes against the person. They may spring from a desire to hurt another person, whether by insulting language or by injury, and in either case may be prompted by a spirit of revenge, as when someone attacks his enemy. Or the motive may be to secure something belonging to another, as when a robber attacks a traveler, or to forestall some evil, as when one attacks a person of whom one is afraid. Again, crime may be motivated by envy, as when a person in wretched circumstances envies one more fortunate, or one who is successful in an enterprise jealously injures another because he fears the other will catch up with him, or is chagrined because that person already has. Or it may simply be pleasure in the misfortunes of others that tempts people to crime: this is the pleasure felt by those who watch gladiators and anyone who laughs and mocks other people.[1]

These are the chief kinds of sin, which sprout from a craving for domination, or for watching shows, or for sensory pleasure, or from any two of these, or all three together. The consequence is an evil life in opposition to that other "three plus seven," the ten-stringed harp, your Decalogue, O God most high and most sweet.[2]

CONFESSIONS III.8.16

3 In this sermon, delivered in Carthage in October 419, Augustine encourages his congregation to take responsibility for their actions. He is preaching on the text of Saint Paul: "For it is not the good that I want to do that I do, but the evil I do not want to do, that is what I do...." (Romans 7:15–25).

4 This passage, which is part of Augustine's account of his own conversion, affirms his belief that our choices are the exercise of our free (though wounded) will. Choices are often difficult. Our wills are often fragmented, disintegrated. But this drama is part of our human condition, weakened by what Augustine calls original sin. We are not the passive victims of the evil force in the universe, as the Manicheans taught. We do, however, suffer the lasting effects of the original sin, committed in Eden by Adam and Eve. The idea of original sin and its lasting effects is central in Augustine's theology and in much Christian teaching, both Protestant and Catholic. Salvation in Christian understanding consists in being freed from original sin and its consequences.

This lust is not, you see—and this is a point you really must listen to above all else: you see, this lust is not some kind of alien nature, as the ravings of the Manichees would have it. It's our debility, it's our vice. It won't be detached from us and exist somewhere else, but it will be cured and not exist anywhere at all.[3]

Sermon 151.3

When I was making up my mind to serve the Lord my God at last, as I had long since purposed, I was the one who wanted to follow that course, and I was the one who wanted not to. I was the only one involved. I neither wanted it wholeheartedly nor turned from it wholeheartedly. I was at odds with myself, and fragmenting myself.[4] This disintegration was occurring without my consent, but what it indicated was not the presence in me of a mind belonging to some alien nature but the punishment undergone by my own. In this sense, and this sense only, it was not I who brought it about, but the sin that dwelt within me as penalty for that other sin committed with great freedom; for I was a son of Adam.

Confessions VIII.10.22

[~] We reviewed Augustine's teaching about original sin in the Introduction (pages xxviii–xxx). Today, many Christians and Jews do not accept a literal interpretation of the Genesis story of Adam and Eve and their sin against God. And people of all faiths might find objectionable Augustine's identification of sex and procreation as the avenue through which sin travels across generations. But the central point in Augustine's theology of original sin remains plausible: moral ignorance and weakness seems endemic in the human race. In light of contemporary methods in anthropology, psychology, biology, and other disciplines, we might reflect quite differently on the origination and persistence of ignorance and evil in human history. Yet, Augustine's key question remains relevant: why do people behave so badly generation after generation; and how can such behavior be changed and the human condition healed?

[1] In this passage, Augustine distinguishes between the two types of sin: original sin passed on through the generations of human nature and inherited at birth; and personal sins that we repeat and habituate throughout our lives. Today, we might say that both nature and nurture contribute to bad behavior. The combination of the two results in a powerful force—not a cosmic evil such as the Manicheans imagined, but a propensity for moral evil rooted deeply in the human race. A quick review of the past century, including two world wars, the Holocaust, the Khmer Rouge, nuclear and biological weapons, the Balkans, apartheid, racial divides, Soviet gulags, a billion people always hungry, and uncountable crimes and injustices around the globe cry out for some explanation of human cruelty. We could each add our own personal examples of how the greed or lust or power of another has worked its harm in our own lives. Even if one thinks of Augustine's theology of original sin as too pessimistic, he must be given credit for taking human sin and suffering seriously and trying to probe its origins.

☐ Original Sin

Sin ... comes from the passing on of mortality and the constant repetition of sensual pleasure. The former derives from the punishment for the original sin, the latter from the punishment for repeated sin; with the former we are born into this life, while the latter we augment over the course of our lives. These two things, which we may call nature and habit, create a very strong and unconquerable covetousness once they have been joined together, which [Paul] refers to as sin and says dwells in his flesh—that is, possesses a certain sovereignty and rule, as it were.[1]

MISCELLANY OF QUESTIONS IN RESPONSE TO SIMPLICIAN 1.10

2 Augustine was careful to say that original sin does not destroy our free will, but does weaken it. Original sin is not an ethical escape hatch: we are responsible for the evil that we do.

3 God does not abandon us to this weakened state. According to Augustine's theology of grace, which we shall explore shortly, God provides the clarity we need to know what is right and good, as well as the strength needed to do it.

4 Note again Augustine's emphasis on sin as a choice.

5 This passage shows how Augustine developed his theology of original sin. Besides the guilt of Adam and Eve, which we all carry, their sin wounded our human nature in two ways: ignorance (we do not know what is the right and good thing to do); and weakness (we find no joy or delight in doing what is right and good). As Augustine explains it, God's grace operates in us in two ways: enlightening our minds in knowing the good, and delighting our hearts in doing it.

6 In our sins we repeat the origin of all sin: pride, which is putting ourselves in God's place as Adam and Eve did.

7 This is a very direct summary of Augustine's theology of sin and original sin taken from one of his sermons in the year 417. In this address, he is explaining sin to the congregation to help them distinguish moral responsibility from the Manichean idea of cosmic evil.

For willing itself is in our power since it is close at hand, but the fact that doing the good is not in our power is part of the deserts of the original sin.[2] For nothing remains of this first nature of humankind but the punishment of sin, through which mortality itself has become a kind of second nature, and it is from this that the grace of the Creator frees those who have submitted to him through faith.[3]

MISCELLANY OF QUESTIONS IN RESPONSE TO SIMPLICIAN 1.11

Since a human being can be without sin in this life, when God's grace helps the human will, I could easily and truthfully give as an answer to the question why no one is without sin: because he does not will to be.[4] But if someone asks me why he does not will to be, the question becomes a long one. I will, nonetheless, give a short answer to it, without precluding a more careful investigation. Human beings do not will to do what is right, either because they do not know whether it is right or because they find no delight in it.[5] For we will something with greater strength in proportion to the certainty of our knowledge of its goodness and the deep delight that we find in it. Ignorance and weakness, then, are defects that hinder the will from being moved to do a good deed or to refrain from an evil deed.... Consequently, do not attribute to God the cause of any human sin. The cause of all human failings is, after all, pride.[6]

THE PUNISHMENT AND FORGIVENESS OF SINS AND THE BAPTISM OF LITTLE ONES II.17.26, 27

What, at the present moment, are the evils of humanity? Error and weakness. Either you don't know what to do, and you go wrong, you fall into error; or else you know what should be done, and you are overpowered by weakness. So every human evil is error and weakness.[7]

SERMON 182.6

1 The delight, attraction, and influence of the world around us is good and natural. How we respond, appropriately or inordinately, makes the moral difference.

2 This is a very interesting observation. There is nothing inherently wrong with authority and power. But it often goes very wrong for the reasons Augustine elaborates here. One wonders if his analysis of the abuse of power is autobiographical, reflecting on what he observed, or even practiced, in the imperial court in Milan, or later among his fellow bishops.

3 Here, Augustine mentions explicitly the order inherent in loving. Greater love is due to "higher" realities of greater complexity and subtlety. The next sentence mentions friendship—certainly a human reality of great complexity, subtlety, and unity. Friendship was very important to Augustine, and he writes about it at length in *Confessions*, as we shall see. Disordered loving can destroy friendship when we value the things our friends may have above who they are in themselves as persons.

4 In the hierarchy of being, God is the infinite fullness of being. Augustine teaches that our love of all the beautiful and good things and persons that God has created is best understood and practiced in light of the Infinite One who sustains all creation in being. To love a thing or a person in light of God is not to diminish their inherent beauty or goodness. It is to put all things and persons in the ultimate context of the possibility of their very existence—which is God.

☐ The Disorder in Sin

The beautiful form of material things attracts our eyes, so we are drawn to gold, silver, and the like. We are powerfully influenced by the feel of things agreeable to the touch; and each of our other senses finds some quality that appeals to it individually in the variety of material objects.[1] There is the same appeal in worldly rank, and the possibility it offers of commanding and dominating other people: this too holds its attraction, and often provides an opportunity for settling old scores.[2] We may seek all these things, O Lord, but in seeking them we must not deviate from your law. The life we live here is open to temptation by reason of a certain measure and harmony between its own splendor and all these beautiful things of low degree.[3] Again, the friendship that draws human beings together in a tender bond is sweet to us because out of many minds it forges a unity. Sin gains entrance through these and similar things when we turn to them with immoderate desire, since they are the lowest kinds of goods and we thereby turn away from the better and higher: from yourself, O Lord our God, and your truth and your law. These lowest goods hold delights for us indeed, but no such delights as does my God, who made all things; for in him the just man finds delight, and for upright souls he himself is joy (see Psalm 63:11).[4]

CONFESSIONS II.5.10

5   Note Augustine's insistence on the good of the whole person: body and soul. He rejects the Manichean teaching that the physical world and the human body were part of cosmic evil. But Augustine does maintain a Neoplatonic hierarchy, which affirms that our capacity for thought, reflection, and choice is higher than our physical experience. Fifth-century thinkers did not have the advantages of contemporary neuroscience that stresses the interdependence of mind and body. Contemporary theologians may avoid Platonic dualism by reflecting on the soul as the expression of the highest complexity of our human being.

6   Augustine often speaks of Jesus Christ as a physician—*Christus Medicus* in Latin—who heals us of the effects of original sin and of our personal sins, namely ignorance and weakness.

➤   Augustine's searing realism about human sinfulness is balanced by repeated affirmations throughout his writings about the goodness of creation. God made all things and all things are good (Genesis 1:31). Part of the joy of being human is to delight in the glories of creation and their delightful play upon our senses. We are called to love and enjoy all creation.

However, there are degrees of love, according to Augustine. There is an order in loving. We do not love our pet in the same way we love our child. We should love all things in light of their being created by God.

Sin enters the economy of love when love's inherent order is violated, when the hierarchy of loves is inverted. Because of ignorance or weakness or habit, we love inordinately and immoderately. Natural passion becomes obsession. Delight becomes destructive. Desire overwhelms reason and justice.

God is the maker of all creatures. But every creature of God is good, and every human being, insofar as he is a human being and not insofar as he is a sinner, is a creature. God, therefore, is the creator of the human body and soul. Neither of these is evil and neither is hated by God, for he hates nothing that he has made.[5] The soul, however, is more excellent than the body, but God the author and creator of each is more excellent than both soul and body, and he hates nothing in the human being other than sin. Sin, however, is a disorder and a perversion in the human being—that is, a turning away from the Creator, who is more excellent, and a turning to created things, which are inferior.

MISCELLANY OF QUESTIONS IN RESPONSE TO SIMPLICIAN 2.18

Human nature was in the beginning created blameless and without any defect. But that human nature, in which each of us is born of Adam, now needs a physician, because it is not in good health.[6] All the goods that it has in its constitution—life, the senses, and the mind—it has from the sovereign God, its creator and maker. But the defect that darkens and weakens those natural goods so that there is need for enlightenment and healing did not come from its blameless maker. It came from the original sin, which was committed by free choice.

NATURE AND GRACE 3.3

◥ In Book II of *Confessions,* Augustine introduces a question to which he often returns not only in this book but in many other writings as well. The question in Latin is *unde malum?* Whence evil? If God is good, and all that God created is good, where does evil come from?

This question is related to sin and its origins, but goes deeper. If one accepts Augustine's theology of original sin, one can still ask, "But why did Adam and Eve choose to disobey God in the first place?" The scriptural answer is that they were tempted. But why the temptation? Why did certain angels choose to rebel against God? *Unde malum?*

The Manicheans had a ready answer to this question, and Augustine accepted their answer, at least for a while. Evil is an equal and opposite force in the cosmos, which they named *Hyle.* It is coeternal with God. In this universe, the lighter, spiritual form of matter that is good is mixed in with the darker, heavier form of matter that is *Hyle.*

In *Confessions,* Augustine spends a good deal of time refuting Manichean teaching. In Book II, he tells the story of a prank that he and some teenage friends pulled one warm summer evening when they stole pears from a tree in a neighbor's orchard. Augustine goes on for pages analyzing this memory, using it to reflect on the nature of evil. His philosophical conclusion is that evil is not a creation of God. In fact, in itself it is *nothing.* It is an absence of good.

1 Note the symbolism in the tree. It reminds the reader of the tree in the garden of Eden, the scene of the original sin.

2 Augustine introduces the idea of decay—of slow disintegration into nothing. His rather harsh self-critique provides a context within which to develop his theme of nothingness.

3 Notice how he personifies his crime by addressing it personally; then he reduces it to nothingness. In this and the following passage, the word "nothing" (*nihil* in Latin), or a variation of it (all italicized for emphasis), appears over and over. This literary repetition stresses Augustine's philosophical notion of evil as nothing.

☐ The Nature of Evil

Close to our vineyard there was a pear tree laden with fruit.[1] This fruit was not enticing, either in appearance or in flavor. We nasty lads went there to shake down the fruit and carry it off at dead of night, after prolonging our games out of doors until that late hour according to our abominable custom. We took enormous quantities, not to feast on ourselves but perhaps to throw to the pigs; we did eat a few, but that was not our motive: we derived pleasure from the deed simply because it was forbidden.

Look upon my heart, O God, look upon this heart of mine, on which you took pity in its abysmal depths. Enable my heart to tell you now what it was seeking in this action, which made me bad for no reason, in which there was no motive for my malice except malice. The malice was decay: not with the thing for which I was falling into decay but with decay itself, for I was depraved in soul, and I leapt down from your strong support into destruction, hungering not for some advantage to be gained by the foul deed, but for the foulness of it.[2]

CONFESSIONS II.4.9

What did I love in you, O my theft, what did I love in you, the nocturnal crime of my sixteenth year? There was *nothing* beautiful about you, for you were *nothing* but a theft. Are you really *anything* at all, for me to be speaking to you like this [italics mine]?[3]

CONFESSIONS II.6.12

4 The adolescent "gang mentality" that Augustine remembers from his youth is a diminished or, to use Augustine's word, a "decayed" form of friendship. So in this petty crime, *nothing* was gained; *no one* profited; there was even *no* motive.

5 The "stupid deceivers" are the Manicheans.

6 The origin of evil was a real, pressing philosophical question for the young Augustine. He never really answers it, beyond his claim that evil does not come from God and so is *no-thing*. In a sense, the origins of evil are shrouded in the mystery of creation itself. While he always presses for a rational explanation of the ultimate questions that arise on the journey of faith, Augustine is also willing to acknowledge mystery when he cannot probe its depths—like Job before the mystery of God (Job 42:1–6). In like manner, Augustine accepts the limits of thought with regard to his own origin: "I do not know where I came from" (*Confessions* I,6,7); and even with regard to his own motivations: "I had become a great enigma to myself " (*Confessions* IV.4, 9).

A problem with Augustine's philosophy of evil is that the existential effects of evil are quite real. To describe the Holocaust as an inherently evil event is one thing. But to say that such evil in itself is ultimately nothingness or simply the absence of good risks dismissing the reality of the suffering. Augustine's theology of sin is more appropriate for reflecting on a moral evil such as the Holocaust.

What fruit did I ever reap from those things, which I now blush to remember, and especially from that theft in which I found *nothing* to love save the theft itself, wretch that I was? It was *nothing*, and by the very act of committing it I became more wretched still. And yet, as I recall my state of mind at the time, I would not have done it alone; I most certainly would not have done it alone. It follows, then, that I also loved the camaraderie with my fellow thieves. So it is not true to say that I loved *nothing* other than the theft? Ah, but it is true, because that gang mentality too was a *nothing*.... What an exceedingly unfriendly form of friendship that was! It was a seduction of the mind hard to understand, which instilled into me a craving to do harm for sport and fun. I was greedy for another person's loss without any desire on my part to gain something or to settle a score. Let the others only say, "Come on, let's go and do it!" and I am ashamed to hold back from the shameless act [italics mine].**4**

CONFESSIONS II.8.16; 9.17

I was being subtly maneuvered into accepting the views of those stupid deceivers by the questions they constantly asked me about the origin of evil....**5** I did not know that evil is nothing but the diminishment of good to the point where *nothing* at all is left [italics mine].

CONFESSIONS III.7.12

Where, then, is evil; where does it come from and how did it creep in? What is its root, its seed? Or does it not exist at all? But in that case, why do we fear and avoid something that has no reality?... Either the evil we fear exists, or our fear itself is the evil. So where does it come from, if the good God made all things good? He is the greater good, to be sure, the supreme good, and the things he has made are lesser goods; nonetheless Creator and creatures are all good. Whence, then, comes evil?... Such thoughts as these was I turning over in my miserable soul, weighed down as it was by the gnawing anxieties that flowed from my fear that death might overtake me before I had found the truth.**6**

CONFESSIONS VII.5.7

7   This is another reference to the order or hierarchy of creation. Everything created is good, but some things are "more good."

Everything that exists is good, then; and so evil, the source of which I was seeking, cannot be a substance, because if it were, it would be good. Either it would be an indestructible substance, and that would mean it was very good indeed, or it would be a substance liable to destruction—but then it would not be destructible unless it were good.

I saw, then, for it was made clear to me, that you have made all good things, and that there are absolutely no substances that you have not made. I saw, too, that you have not made all things equal.[7] They all exist because they are severally good but collectively very good, for our God has made all things *exceedingly good* (Genesis 1:31).

For you, evil has no being at all, and this is true not of yourself only, but of everything you have created, since apart from you there is nothing that could burst in and disrupt the order you have imposed on it.

CONFESSIONS VII.12.18; 13.19

◥ We return now to the theme of the will, weakened by original sin. Augustine uses the story of his own faith struggle to illustrate his theology. This last passage before Augustine's conversion stresses the impotence of the human will and our absolute need for God's grace. This is the paradox inherent in Augustine's understanding of free will. We are called to make choices, by our very nature and God's design. Yet we are deeply wounded creatures who struggle mightily to make those choices that define us. In fact, without God's help we are incapable of making or sustaining those choices. In front of an important decision we are "dismayed," "breathless," "left hanging," even though we know what it is we should do. Augustine is setting up the reader to understand the need for God's grace to help the will choose the right and the good.

[1] As the moment of his conversion approaches, his exercise of will in decision making, Augustine's language grows ever more dramatic. Imagine yourself listening to Augustine or some other professional reader dramatizing these pages in a public reading of *Confessions*. That is how most people would have first experienced this text in Augustine's time and for centuries thereafter.

[2] Note the anti-Manichean insistence here that the struggle is all Augustine's, not any cosmic battle between good and evil.

☐ Paralysis of Will

"Let it be now," I was saying to myself. "Now is the moment, let it be now," and merely by saying this I was moving toward the decision. I would almost achieve it, but then fall just short; yet I did not slip right down to my starting point, but stood aside to get my breath back. Then I would make a fresh attempt, and now I was almost there, almost there ... I was touching the goal, grasping it ... and then I was not there, not touching, not grasping it. I shrank from dying to death and living to life, for ingrained evil was more powerful in me than new-grafted good. The nearer it came, that moment when I would be changed, the more it pierced me with terror. Dismayed, but not quite dislodged, I was left hanging....[1]

All this argument in my heart raged only between myself and myself.[2] Alypius stood fast at my side, silently awaiting the outcome of my unprecedented agitation....

3 Scholars are uncertain as to whether there was actually a fig tree in the garden. Augustine may be exercising literary license and alluding once again to scriptural image. Adam and Eve, after their sin of disobedience in the garden of Eden, use fig leaves to cover their shame (Genesis 3:7). Jesus curses a sterile fig tree, which then dies (Matthew 21:19)—perhaps symbolic of the old self in Augustine that needs to die. Nathaniel is called down by Jesus from his perch in a fig tree to follow him (John 1:47–48). As we have seen, for Augustine it is the sin of Adam and Eve in the garden that is the cause of our wounded will.

4 Augustine still stands in need of God's grace so that he can exercise his free will and make his decision.

But as this deep meditation dredged all my wretchedness up from the secret profundity of my being and heaped it all together before the eyes of my heart, a huge storm blew up within me and brought on a heavy rain of tears. In order to pour them out unchecked with the sobs that accompanied them, I arose and left Alypius, for solitude seemed to me more suitable for the business of weeping. I withdrew far enough to ensure that his presence—even his—would not be burdensome to me. This was my need, and he understood it, for I think I had risen to my feet and blurted out something, my voice already choked with tears. He accordingly remained, in stunned amazement, at the place where we had been sitting. I flung myself down somehow under a fig tree and gave free rein to the tears that burst from my eyes like rivers, as an acceptable sacrifice to you.[3] Many things I had to say to you, and the gist of them, though not the precise words, was: "O Lord, how long? How long? Will you be angry forever? Do not remember our age-old sins" (Psalm 78:5, 8). For by these I was conscious of being held prisoner. I uttered cries of misery: "Why must I go on saying, 'Tomorrow ... tomorrow'? Why not now? Why not put an end to my depravity this very hour?"[4]

CONFESSIONS VIII.11.25, 27, 28

1 Augustine uses this quote from Proverbs many times in his arguments against Pelagian thinking. Augustine believes that we choose to do the right and the good thing ultimately because we love it; we find delight in doing it. Since God is love, according to John's First Letter, it is God's dwelling within our very souls that is the source of our love for the right and the good. God's love prepares our wills.

2 Pelagius, and later Julian, accuse Augustine of denying free will and so "dehumanizing" the person. Augustine consistently responds by affirming that free will is of the very essence of human nature. Our will is profoundly weakened by original sin, and by our own habits of sin—but it is not destroyed. It needs God's healing, saving grace.

3 Augustine sees God's help extending through all phases of human choice and action. To use a modern distinction, one might think about Augustine's understanding of human motivation as more akin to psychoanalytic thought. We are complicated, complex beings who operate out of many levels and layers of conscious and unconscious forces, stresses, and memories. God's grace operates and heals at every level as we strive to do the right and the good.

Pelagius's approach is simpler, more like a behavioral psychologist. You determine what behavior is desirable, and then work to modify and accomplish your goal. God illumines and inspires us about the proper behavior to do the right and the good. We take it from there.

It is helpful to remember that Augustine's theology of grace emerged from his own conversion struggle. He also lived among and served the common folk of his diocese. He knew from firsthand experience how difficult it was for ordinary people to do the right thing consistently. By contrast, Pelagius moved in the upper classes of society and among ascetics and monks. Although Augustine's approach seems to emphasize our dependence upon God, Augustine believed God's grace was available to us, especially to those who struggle with moral decisions. In the end, Pelagius' approach requires a superhuman effort of will, of which only an ascetic religious and social elite think themselves capable.

☐ Saved by Grace:
The Pelagian Controversy

Each person obeys the commandments of God ... only with love....
Only God gives this love, for love come from God (1 John 4:7). *The will
is prepared by the Lord* (Proverbs 8:35)....[1]

UNFINISHED WORK IN ANSWER TO JULIAN III.114

After all, who does not know that no one believes except by free choice
of the will? But the will is prepared by the Lord, nor is the will
completely rescued from its evil servitude, which is due to its merits
except when it is prepared by the Lord through gratuitous grace....[2]
The free choice of a human being that is inborn and absolutely unable
to be lost is that by which all will to be happy, even those who do not
will those things that lead to happiness.

UNFINISHED WORK IN ANSWER TO JULIAN VI.10, 11

Hence, with regard to this question about God's grace and help, pay
attention to those three factors that he [Pelagius] distinguished with
perfect clarity: the power, the willing, and the being, that is, the ability,
the will, and the action. Let him, then, agree with us that God helps not
merely the ability in human beings, even if they do not will or act well,
but also the will and the action, that is, so that we will and act in the
right way, which are present in human beings only when they will and
act well.[3] Let him, as I said, agree that God also helps the will and the
action and helps them in such a way that we will or do nothing good
without that help, and let him agree that this is the grace of God
through Jesus Christ our Lord, by which he makes us righteous with his

4 In Augustine's opinion, Pelagius and those who thought like him were justifying themselves before God and so did not really need Christ's saving grace. So Augustine, and eventually the official church, declared their teaching heretical.

5 Early in his controversy with Pelagius, Augustine worked patiently to identify what was at the heart of their disagreement, hoping that Pelagius would understand all the implications of his thought and change his mind.

6 This is a lovely summary statement of Augustine's theology of grace. God's Word enlightens our minds to know the good, and God's Spirit moves our hearts to take delight in doing it.

You may notice that these first two passages are from a book with a strange title. Augustine finished his *Confessions* and the dramatic story of his conversion around the year 400. Almost thirty years later, as a bishop in his midseventies (quite old for the fifth century), Augustine was engaged in a heated exchange of books and letters with a young, upstart bishop from southern Italy by the name of Julian. This bishop had taken up the cause of Pelagius. He attacked Augustine and the teaching of original sin with a zeal and ferocity that often got very personal—he even insulted Monica by recalling the incident recounted in Augustine's *Confessions* about her drinking too much wine as a girl (IX.8.17,18).

This book was Augustine's response, point by point, to Julian's arguments. Unfinished when Augustine died in 430, it is nonetheless a massive tome.

own righteousness, not with ours, so that it is our true righteousness that comes to us from him.**4** Then no point of controversy will, as far as I can see, be left between us regarding the help of God's grace.**5**

The Grace of Christ and Original Sin I.47.52

This grace not only makes us know what we should do, but also makes us do what we know; it not only makes us believe what we should love, but makes us love what we believe.**6**

The Grace of Christ and Original Sin I.12.13

Pelagius has to distinguish knowledge and love,... Each of them is a gift of God, but the one is a smaller, the other a greater gift. He ... attributes the smaller of these two gifts to divine help, while he wrongly claims the greater for human choice.

The Grace of Christ and Original Sin I.26.27

✎ *Confessions* was written at least ten years before Augustine became involved in his argument with Pelagius and later Julian. But as we have seen, Augustine's theology of grace is a prominent and recurring theme in *Confessions*. He believes that God's grace empowers us to accomplish whatever it is that God calls us to do. The context for this bold claim by Augustine on God is the infinite love that God has for each and every one of us.

1 Pelagius was living in Rome around 404 or 405 when he first heard this sentence being quoted from Augustine's *Confessions*. He strongly objected. Augustine repeats the phrase, "Give what you command and command what you will" four times in Book X—so Pelagius could hardly have missed it!

This phrase grated against Pelagius's fundamental belief in the power of the human will to accomplish what it set out to do. He was writing a book at that time on the letters of Saint Paul in which he was giving his own interpretation of divine grace as primarily initial inspiration and enlightenment for the benefit of the believer, who would then carry out what God wanted on the strength of his or her own willpower. He saw in Augustine's radical theology of grace a denial of free will.

2 For Augustine, living out the virtue of continence, that is, living a chaste and celibate life, was the one thing he wanted to do, and which he thought God was calling him to do, but before which he felt altogether helpless.

3 Augustine is quoting from the Hebrew Bible apocryphal Book of Wisdom. The text calls for the believer to acknowledge God's grace in the practice of chastity.

4 In this sentence, Augustine is referring to the hierarchy of beings, or one might call it the hierarchy of loving, in which God is to be loved in and through all other orders of creation.

☐ Give What You Command

On your exceedingly great mercy rests all my hope. Give what you command, and then command whatever you will.[1] You order us to practice continence.[2] A certain writer tells us, *I knew that no one can be continent except by God's gift, and that it is already a mark of wisdom to recognize whose gift this is* (Wisdom 8:21).[3] By continence, the scattered elements of the self are collected and brought back into the unity from which we have slid away into dispersion; for anyone who loves something else along with you, but does not love it for your sake, loves you less.[4] O Love, ever burning, never extinguished, O Charity, my God, set me on fire! You command continence: give what you command, and then command whatever you will.

CONFESSIONS X.29.40

59

5 This last sentence must be read in the context of the richness and fullness of Augustine's understanding of love. This includes love of God, neighbor, and self, as elaborated in Jesus's words from the New Testament. Love is also ordered in that we love and relate to all persons and all creation in and through God's love for us and our love for God. So Augustine believes that when we live grounded in the reality of God's love, our actions will be supported by God's grace, and will advance God's ongoing work of creation through our own works of love.

In another of his *Homilies on the First Epistle of John*, Augustine expresses his belief in the power and purpose of love even more directly: "Love, and do what you want" (7.8). This is one of Augustine's most quoted phrases. A proper understanding of Augustine's meaning is clear when you consider the context.

You shall love the Lord your God from your whole heart, and from your whole soul, and from your whole mind, and you shall love your neighbor as yourself. On these two commandments the whole law depends, and also the prophets (Matthew 22:33, 39–40). See, the whole of this epistle speaks of these commandments. Hold onto love, then, and be secure. Why do you fear that you might do something bad to someone? Who does anything bad to someone that he loves? If you love, nothing can happen apart from doing good.[5]

HOMILIES ON THE FIRST EPISTLE OF JOHN 10.7

1 In Latin, the phrase, "take up and read" is rendered *tolle, lege*. This is another famous Augustinian quote. God's grace comes to Augustine through taking and reading the scriptures. This would be the continuing pattern of his life: God's grace and presence would heal and support Augustine's faith through his lifelong engagement with sacred scripture.

2 This practice of opening a book of scripture at random and alighting upon a specific text appears elsewhere in Christian antiquity as a way of discerning God's will. Augustine mentions such an event in the life of the Egyptian monk Antony, for whom scripture was also the defining moment of grace in his conversion.

3 What a powerful verb to describe divine grace: Augustine was "stung" into action, as if by the sting of a divine bee! Bees symbolize industry and order—getting things done—which was the opposite of Augustine's inaction so far. Bees also call to mind the Promised Land that flows with milk and honey.

4 This is the defining moment of grace in Augustine's journey of faith. His future will not always be easy and smooth as he continues on his pilgrimage of grace. But he knows that God will be with him.

~ Augustine's conversion is the climax of his *Confessions*. He will go on to Book IX, which recounts the story of Monica's death; to Book X, on memory; and to Books XI through XIII, in which he elaborates themes from the biblical book of Genesis. But it is his conversion of heart, so dramatically described in Book VIII, which provides the key to understanding *Confessions* as a whole.

At the literary and theological center of Augustine's *Confessions* is his profound, personal conviction that our will to believe is possible only by God's grace. Augustine's theology of grace became normative for subsequent Christian teaching—though not in all of its colorful detail, as we shall see. Church councils convened in the centuries after Augustine's death continued to debate and refine how Christians understand the subtle relationship between God's grace and human effort.

☐ Conversion

I went on talking like this and weeping in the intense bitterness of my broken heart. Suddenly I heard a voice from a house nearby—perhaps a voice of some boy or girl, I do not know—singing over and over again, "Pick it up and read, pick it up and read."[1] My expression immediately altered, and I began to think hard whether children ordinarily repeated a ditty like this in any sort of game, but I could not recall ever having heard it anywhere else. I stemmed the flood of tears and rose to my feet, believing that this could be nothing other than a divine command to open the book and read the first passage I chanced upon;[2] for I had heard the story of how Antony had been instructed by a Gospel text. He happened to arrive while the Gospel was being read, and took the words to be addressed to himself when he heard, *Go and sell all you possess and give the money to the poor: you will have treasure in heaven. Then come, follow me* (Matthew 19:21). So he was promptly converted to you by this plainly divine message. Stung into action,[3] I returned to the place where Alypius was sitting, for on leaving it I had put down there the book of the apostle's letters. I snatched it up, opened it, and read in silence the passage on which my eyes first lighted: *Not in dissipation and drunkenness, nor in debauchery and lewdness, nor in arguing and jealousy; but put on the Lord Jesus Christ, and make no provision for the flesh or the gratification of your desires* (Romans 13:13–14). I had no wish to read further, nor was there need. No sooner had I reached the end of the verse than the light of certainty flooded my heart and all dark shards of doubt fled away.[4]

CONFESSIONS VIII.12.29

◥ In the Introduction (pages xiii–xlii), we reviewed Augustine's thinking about predestination. It is a theological tool he used to sharpen his teaching about divine grace against the Pelagian school of theology. Our wills are strengthened and we do good only because God's grace inclines our wills and moves our hearts to love the good. Augustine argues that it is completely and only God's choice as to whom such grace is given. Only certain ones are chosen, predestined for grace.

As we have seen, this theological argument for predestination rests on several scriptural quotes that speak about our destiny as God's decision: Ephesians 1:5, 11; 2 Timothy 1:9; and Matthew 20:23. It ignores 1 Timothy 2:4, which claims that God wills everyone to be saved.

Augustine himself, as a pastor, advised that predestination should not be brought up with common folk, but that a preacher should simply encourage the faithful to persevere in faith, hope, and love. Predestination is still found as a received doctrine among some Christian denominations, which quote the same scriptural texts that Augustine used.

1 This work *The Gift of Perseverance* is part of another work entitled *On the Predestination of the Saints*, which Augustine wrote toward the very end of his life in 428 or 429.

2 This sermon was preached sometime between 417 and 419, probably in Hippo, on the text of Romans 8:30–33. It shows Augustine's more pastoral commentary on the theme.

3 This is a great summary of how Augustine approaches religion and grace. Religion is not a matter of God rewarding good people who keep the commandments and live good lives (which is probably most people's understanding of any religion). It is rather that God loves people into being good and doing good—despite themselves.

☐ Predestination

God's grace is not given in accordance with our merits.... Final perseverance is not given except by him who has predestined us for his kingdom and glory.[1]

THE GIFT OF PERSEVERANCE 21.55

Let all of us then, my brothers and sisters, take a look at ourselves inside, weigh ourselves up, test ourselves in all our deeds, our good works, to see which ones we do with love and for love, not expecting any temporal reward, but only God's promise, the sight of God's face.... So if the faith that works through love is in you, you already belong to the predestined, the called, the justified; so see that it grows in you. The faith, after all, that works through love cannot exist without hope.... *We are God's children*, predestined, called, justified; *we are God's children, and it has not yet appeared what we shall be* (1 John 3:2).[2]

SERMON 158.7

Those who do have faith, though, believe by God's grace; they mustn't pride themselves on it. It's a gift from God. Is the reason God chose us, do you suppose, that we were good? He didn't choose good people, but people he wished to make good.[3]

SERMON 229F.1

◥ In the final years of his long life, Augustine undertook a review of all his many writings. This work is called *Reconsiderations,* and in it Augustine notes where he would modify or amend various parts of his books (he never got to a review of his sermons and letters).

This is a remarkable source text for tracking Augustine's books and for understanding the contexts of his many works, as Augustine himself did. It is also remarkable for the intellectual humility and self-criticism Augustine exercised. This quote from *The Gift of Perseverance* reflects these characteristics of the old bishop as he looks back on his life's work.

Augustine was a religious leader who constantly encouraged others to think for themselves and to challenge him when they thought he was wrong. For Augustine, the life of the mind is a restless quest for truth and an essential part of the pilgrimage of faith. His bracing arguments with the Manicheans and the Pelagians show how seriously he took questions about free will, human sinfulness, God's grace, and healing. But paragraphs like the one above show how he refused to canonize his own thought, and how important continued reflection and open dialogue are in our common search for truth. He continues to be a worthy partner for contemporary seekers of truth to engage along their spiritual journeys.

1 This paragraph, toward the end of a long tract on predestination, is reminiscent of a similar invitation to the reader in *The Trinity* I.1.5 (see page 7). Augustine will argue his points with great conviction and rhetorical power, but he remains open to dialogue.

2 He was working on *Reconsiderations* at the same time he was writing *The Gift of Perseverance.*

3 This is another example of the Augustinian understanding of humility as truth and honesty about oneself.

4 One thinks of *Sermon* 169.18, quoted on page 5 of this book. The journey of faith does not lead to a goal or end in this life. The pilgrimage in search of truth lasts until our final day, and requires a spiritual openness and intellectual hospitality that grows as we age.

☐ Reconsideration

And yet, I would not want anyone to embrace all my views in order to be my follower, but only those points on which he sees that I am not mistaken.[1] For I am now writing the books in which I have undertaken to review my works in order to show that I have not always held the same views;[2] rather, I think that, as I wrote, I made progress by the mercy of God, but not that I started off with perfection. For I speak with more arrogance than truth if I say that I have now at this age come to perfection without any error in my writing.[3] But it makes a difference how much and on what issues one is in error and how easily one is corrected or with what stubbornness one tries to defend his error. We can, of course, have good hope for someone if the last day of this life finds him making progress so that he receives in addition what was lacking to him as he made progress, and we may judge him worthy of perfection rather than of punishment.[4]

THE GIFT OF PERSEVERANCE 21.55

Part Three:
Intent upon God

Augustine affirms the human capacity to approach the Divine and experience the Creator through the use of our minds and hearts. He believes in the scriptural affirmation that human beings are made in the image of the Divine Being (Genesis 1:31). So he concludes that there must be traces of the Divine in us that allow us to approach God, especially through our intellect and will. All of creation is God's work, and so bespeaks the genius of the Divine Artisan. We can "touch the fringes of the Divine" or "brush up against" the mystery of God in our experience of self, of others, and of the universe.

So Augustine rejects the agnostic tendencies of philosophical skeptics who challenge us to suspend any affirmation of faith. As we have see in Part Two, he also affirms the role of divine grace in opening our minds and drawing our hearts toward the mystery of God. Our minds and hearts are therefore "adequate" to approach the mystery of the Divine, as the medieval theologian Thomas Aquinas would write eight hundred years after Augustine. Nonetheless, Augustine emphasizes that we stand in need of grace to realize the fullness of our divine potential, a process that may begin in this life but which will reach completion only in heaven.

1 Augustine wrote *Soliloquies* (a word he coined meaning "conversations with oneself") shortly after his conversion and before his baptism, while on a retreat in the northern Italian town of Cassiciacum (probably the modern-day Cassago Brianza). This early book is a prayerful conversation between Augustine and his own reason, which is his dialogue partner in the work. They discuss together two topics: knowledge of one's own soul and knowledge of God. For Augustine, these two are inextricably linked.

2 The word for God in Latin is *Deus*, so in the original this passage reads: "*Deus*—what a short word I have uttered, four letters, two syllables! Is that really all that *Deus* is, just four letters and two syllables?"

☐ Knowing God

God, who is always the same, may I know myself, may I know you. That is my prayer.[1]

SOLILOQUIES 2.1.1

Look, I utter a word when I say, "God"; what a short word I have uttered, three letters, one syllable![2] Is that really all that God is, just three letters and one syllable? Or, rather, is what is understood by these letters cherished all the more insofar as the word is so insignificant? What happened in your heart when you heard "God"? What happened in my heart when I was saying "God"? Something great and supreme occurred to our mind; it soars utterly above and beyond every changeable, carnal, and merely natural creature....

3 Augustine loved to comment on the interplay between spoken, audible words and the mental images or ideas they evoke. He was an early "semiologist," interested in the science of signs and symbols. He elaborates at length on the symbolism of words in his work *The Teacher*, a dialogue with his son, Adeodatus, written shortly before or after the boy died in 388 or 389.

He writes that the Word of God, Christ, is within our minds and hearts, teaching us the true meaning of the words that we hear or read from human teachers.

4 There is an influence of Neoplatonic thinking here in the movement from our experience of goodness in the many aspects of creation to the Good Itself, or as Plato had called it, the Idea of the Good, or the Eternal Form of Goodness. Plato's thought influenced Augustine through the third-century philosopher Plotinus, whose work is known as Neoplatonism. The latter emphasized a mystical ascent from this world to the Eternal and Infinite One, illustrated in this Augustinian movement from many goods to the One Good that is God. Neoplatonic thought, which Augustine first encountered in Milan, helped him understand God to be pure spirit.

5 This paragraph comes in the middle of a very long sermon preached around 410. In this sermon, Augustine is about to explain to the congregation an analogy for understanding the Trinity (the analogy of memory, understanding, and will—which we will explore later). But he cautions his listeners to remember, understand, and accept that any analogy or explanation of God is infinitely limited. Augustine's probing, analytical mind was keenly aware of the impossibility of completely knowing or fully comprehending the divine mystery. Our minds, enlightened by grace, can entertain the idea of God; our hearts, moved by grace, can approach God. Nonetheless, when it comes to comprehending the fullness of the Holy One, our thoughts are "quite inadequate to their object, and incapable of grasping God" (*The Trinity* V.1).

So what is that thing in your heart, when you are fixing your mind on some substance that is living, everlasting, almighty, infinite, present everywhere, everywhere whole and entire, nowhere confined? When you fix your mind on all this, there is a word about God in your heart.[3]

HOMILIES ON THE GOSPEL OF JOHN 1.8

The earth is good with its lofty mountains and its folded hills and its level plains, and a farm is good when its situation is pleasant and its land fertile, and a house is good with its harmonious symmetry of architecture so spacious and bright, and animals are good with their animated bodies, and the air is good when mild and salubrious, and food is good when tasty and health-giving, and health is good being without pains or weariness, and a face is good when it has fine proportions and a cheerful expression and a fresh complexion, and the heart of a friend is good with its sweet accord and loving trust, and a just person is good, and riches are good because they are easily put to use, and the sky is good with its sun and moon and stars, and angels are good with their holy obedience, and speech is good as it pleasantly instructs and suitably moves the hearer, and a song is good with its melodious notes and its noble sentiments. Why go on and on? This is good and that is good. Take away this and that and see Good Itself if you can. In this way you will see God, not good with some other good, but the good of every good.... And what is this but God?[4]

THE TRINITY VIII.2.4

So what are we to say about God? If you have fully grasped what you want to say, it isn't God. If you have been able to comprehend it, you have comprehended something else instead of God. If you think you have been able to comprehend, your thoughts have deceived you. So he isn't this, if this is what you have understood; but if he is this, then you haven't understood it. So what is it you want to say, seeing you haven't been able to understand it?[5]

SERMON 52.16

6 | In this sermon, preached around 418, Augustine is instructing his congregation on the opening text of John's Gospel. Augustine is countering the claims of Arianism, a Christian heresy first proposed in the third century by the priest Arius who taught that Jesus was not divine. With the fall of Rome in 410, refugees from Italy were flooding into North Africa, and many of them were Arian Christians. Even in his desire to stress the divinity of Christ, Augustine reminds his people that we cannot presume to understand divinity.

This humility and awe in front of the Eternal and Infinite One runs throughout Augustine's books and sermons on the nature of God. Such humility and theological restraint in front of the Divine is found in other early church writers as well. It has been called apophatic theology in the Greek tradition, or the *via negativa* in the Latin tradition. It affirms that ultimately God is ineffable, that is, not able to be described or spoken of in words. It suggests approaching an understanding of God by suggesting what God is *not*. "It is easier to know what God is *not* than what God is" (*Expositions of the Psalms* 85.12). Similar apophatic theology is found in the Hindu approach to God known as *neti ... neti*: God is "not this" and "not that." Language and conceptualization fail.

Such ignorance is more religious and devout than any presumption of knowledge. After all, we are talking about God. It says, *and the Word was God* (John 1:1).**6** We are talking about God; so why be surprised if you cannot grasp it? I mean, if you can grasp it, it isn't God. Let us rather make a devout confession of ignorance, instead of a brash profession of knowledge. Certainly it is great bliss to have a little touch or taste of God with the mind; but completely to grasp him, to comprehend him, is altogether impossible....

What mind's eye will be able to grasp God, take all of him in? It is enough to touch his fringes, if the mind's eye is pure. But if it does touch upon him, it does so with a kind of immaterial and spiritual touch, but still does not embrace or comprehend him all; and that too, if the mind is pure.

And we human beings are made blessed by our hearts just brushing against that which abides always blessed; and that is itself eternal blessedness; and that by which we are made alive is eternal life; that by which we are made wise is perfect wisdom; that by which we are enlightened is eternal light.

SERMON 117.5

▼ In these three passages, Augustine reveals his own powerful, personal experiences of God's burning love for him and of his yearning love for God. Augustine experienced God not only through his mind, which searched and scoured human philosophy for ways to approach the Divine. The core of Augustine's conversion was an experience of divine love that moved his heart, as he testifies, through the Word of God in Christ and through the grace of God in the Holy Spirit.

The first two of these three selections from *Confessions* are among the most lyrical poetic passages of late Latin literature.

1 Here is another example of the *via negativa*, this time not regarding ideas about God but the felt experience of God. Note, however, that in the following sentences Augustine also affirms the use of analogies in approaching the mystery of God and our experience of the Divine.

2 In Book X of *Confessions*, Augustine explores the role of the senses in Christian spirituality and the experience of God. In a manner unusual among his theological contemporaries, and in anticipation of later Christian mystics, Augustine affirms the goodness and value of our sensory life in our experience of God and in God's approach to us.

3 The last few phrases of this passage are central to understanding Augustine's theology of divine love. God is the active partner who surrounds and embraces Augustine. Earlier in *Confessions* (Book VII), Augustine describes how he strove to approach union with God through the discipline of Neoplatonic mystical ascent to God, the One. These approaches, before his conversion and baptism, were strenuous, tentative, and impossible to sustain (VII.17.23). Augustine teaches that we are created in such a way that we naturally seek God. On our own we may even catch faint glimpses of the Divine, but we falter and lose strength (Book VII). Augustine affirms in faith that sustained relationship with God is possible because God approaches us in love (Book X).

☐ Loving God

But what am I loving when I love you? Not beauty of body nor transient grace, not this fair light, which is now so friendly to my eyes, not melodious song in all its lovely harmonies, not the sweet fragrance of flowers or ointments or spices, not manna or honey, not limbs that draw me to carnal embrace: none of these do I love when I love my God.[1] And yet I do love a kind of light, a kind of voice, a certain fragrance, a food and an embrace, when I love my God:[2] a light, voice, fragrance, food, and embrace for my inmost self, where something limited to no place shines into my mind, where something not snatched away by passing time sings for me, where something no breath blows away yields to me its scent, where there is savor undiminished by famished eating, and where I am clasped in a union from which no satiety can tear me away.[3] This is what I love, when I love my God.

CONFESSIONS X.6.8

4 Augustine is not saying that created realities are not good and unworthy of our love. In his theology of ordered loving he is counseling the need to love each thing according to its nature and purpose, and to love God above all things.

5 This long sentence is a sensuous description of divine grace, powerfully attracting the will to love the God it was created to love.

6 By the time he wrote *Confessions*, Augustine was a very busy bishop administering the affairs of his diocese and addressing the needs of his people, even settling civil disputes for citizens of Hippo. He often complained that his duties kept him from the prayer and reflection that renewed his spirit.

7 Prayer is a "centering" experience, quieting the distracted mind and calming the scattered affections that often keep us from dwelling in and living out of the depths of our being.

8 Throughout his busy life, Augustine occasionally enjoyed mystical experiences of union with God. The mystical dimension of Augustine is often missed by commentators who focus only on his doctrinal arguments and ecclesiastical actions.

Late have I loved you, Beauty so ancient and so new, late have I loved you! Lo, you were within, but I outside, seeking there for you, and upon the shapely things you have made I rushed headlong, I misshapen. You were with me, but I was not with you. They held me back far from you, those things that would have no being were they not in you.[4] You called, shouted, broke through my deafness; you flared, blazed, banished my blindness; you lavished your fragrance, I gasped, and now I pant for you; I tasted you, and I hunger and thirst; you touched me, and I burned for your peace.[5]

CONFESSIONS X.27.38

It is still my constant delight to reflect like this; in such meditation I take refuge from the demand of necessary business, insofar as I can free myself.[6] Nowhere amid all these things that I survey under your guidance do I find a safe haven for my soul except in you; only there are the scattered elements of my being collected, so that no part of me may escape from you.[7]

From time to time you lead me into an inward experience quite unlike any other, a sweetness beyond understanding. If ever it is brought to fullness in me, my life will not be what it is now, though what it will be I cannot tell.[8]

CONFESSIONS X.40.65

◥ As we have seen in the Introduction, Augustine spent almost twenty years composing *The Trinity* (400–19). In this long and difficult treatise of fifteen books, Augustine wrestles with the Christian teaching that the One God is Three Persons: Father, Son, and Holy Spirit, or, in different theological terms, Creator, Redeemer, and Sanctifier. He recalls testimony from scripture about the triune nature of God (Books II to IV) and examines and critiques the writings of other Christian theologians on the topic (Books V to VII).

Augustine introduces his original theology of the Trinity in Book VIII. He suggests that we can see traces of the triune God in various triadic structures in the created world, especially in our experience as human beings, since we are made in God's image. Then from Book IX to Book XV, he elaborates many different triads in human experience, which he claims reflect the triune nature of the Divine Artisan who created us.

1 Throughout *The Trinity*, Augustine frequently reminds his readers that his theological reflections on the triune nature of God are analogies that reflect but do not describe the Holy One. In Augustine's day, as in Saint Paul's, mirrors were of polished, hammered metal. They provided only dark, imperfect, flawed reflections ("puzzling" reflections, in the Latin translation of Saint Paul that Augustine was using). That's how Augustine understood his theological analogies for understanding the Trinity.

2 Augustine proposes the analogy of mind, understanding, and will as the most compelling "trace" of the Trinity in our experience. This human triadic structure is rooted in the heart of the mystery of our intellectual soul or self (*mens* in Latin). These three activities are each distinct from the other, distinguished by the nature of their particular capacity. Yet they exist only in relationship with each other and together comprise one knowing, loving reality (one "substance" in Augustine's terms) that is the rational, living person. Augustine stretches the limits of language in his attempt to invite the reader into the possibility of "glimpsing," however darkly, or "brushing up against," however softly, the mystery of the nature of God, who is three, but One.

☐ God as Trinity

When we think about God the Trinity, we are aware that our thoughts are quite inadequate to their object, and incapable of grasping him as he is; even by someone of the caliber of the apostle Paul, God can only be seen, as it says, *like a puzzling reflection in a mirror* (1 Corinthians 13:12).[1]

The Trinity V.1

These three then, memory, understanding, and will, are not three lives but one life, nor three minds but one mind. So it follows, of course, that they are not three substances but one substance.... In fact, though they are not only each contained by each, they are all contained by each as well. After all, I remember that I have memory and understanding and will, and I understand that I understand and will and remember, and I will that I will and remember and understand, and I remember my whole memory and understanding and will all together.[2]

The Trinity X.4.18

3 | This quote comes from Book XIV as Augustine is bringing his long treatise to a conclusion.

4 | Augustine pushes the analogy further. To this point, his theological exercise has been a long, extended reflection on the triadic structure of the human mind or *mens*. He has been reflecting on the mind itself. In this passage, he takes a transcendent turn. He invites the reader to replace the human mind as the object of theological reflection, and instead to remember, understand, and love God. In this act of faith, the analogy itself deepens and strengthens, and we see a fuller image of God at the center of our souls. When God is the object of our memory, understanding, and love, the human mind moves toward the purpose for which it was made. It is the turn from *knowledge*, which is the mind's attention to created realities (including itself), to *wisdom,* which is the mind's attention to its Creator. Or as Augustine expresses it, we are made to move *through knowledge to wisdom* (*per scientiam ad sapientiam*; Book XII.4.22, 25).

5 | This last sentence brings to mind Augustine's famous sentence from the first paragraph of *Confessions*: "You have made us and drawn us to yourself, and our heart is unquiet until it rests in you."

6 | Augustine returns to his favorite theme of journey here. The Christian's reflection on God is comprised of remembering God, attempting to understand God, and loving God. This threefold process is the pilgrimage of a Christian life. The mystery of the Trinity emerges as the Christian journeys in faith *in Deum*, toward God. This remembering, knowing, and loving God is a process in and by which a believer is "renewed in the recognition of God and in justice and holiness of truth by making progress day by day" (XIV.5.23).

7 | Another caution by Augustine, even after he has developed his theological analogy to its fullest.

Here we are then with the mind remembering itself, understanding itself, loving itself. If we see this, we see a trinity, not yet God, of course, but already the image of God.[3]

This trinity of the mind is not really the image of God because the mind remembers and understands and loves itself, but because it is also able to remember and understand and love him by whom it was made. And when it does this, it becomes wise....[4] Let it then remember its God to whose image it was made and understand and love him. To put it in a word, let the mind worship the uncreated God, by whom it was created with a capacity for him and able to share in him.[5]

As far as we could, we have also used the creation that God made to remind those who ask for reasons in such matters that as far as they can they should descry his invisible things by understanding them through the things that are made, and especially through the rational or intellectual creature that is made to the image of God; so that through this, as a kind of mirror, as far as they can and if they can, they might perceive in our memory, understanding, and will that God is a trinity. Anyone who has a lively intuition of these three (as divinely established in the nature of his mind) and how great a thing it is that his mind has that by which even the eternal and unchanging nature can be recalled, beheld, and desired—it is recalled by memory, beheld by intelligence, embraced by love—has thereby found the image of that supreme Trinity. To the memory, sight, and love of this supreme Trinity, in order to recollect it, see it, and enjoy it, he should refer every ounce and particle of his life.[6] But I have sufficiently warned him, so it seems to me, that this image, made by the trinity and altered for the worse by its own fault, is not so to be compared to that Trinity that it is reckoned similar to it in every respect. Rather, he should note how great the dissimilarity is in whatever similarity there may be.[7]

1 This text is from a homily preached by Augustine at a Christmas midnight Mass, probably sometime after 410. When the Visigoth tribes invaded Rome in 410, thousands of refugees left Italy for the safety of North Africa. They poured into seaport towns like Hippo. This displacement created the social pressures and stresses that accompany exile. However, there was an additional religious dimension to this political migration: a number of the Christians who migrated to Africa from Italy were Arian Christians.

The third- to fourth-century priest Arius, from Alexandria in Egypt, had taught that the Word of God was not eternal and so not divine. Rather, he believed that the Word was created by the Eternal God and thus was not of the same divine substance or being. Subsequent to the emergence of the Word from the eternal Godhead, God created the universe through that Word. This Word became flesh in Jesus, but since the Word itself was not eternal and divine, neither was Jesus.

Arius's teaching was roundly condemned by the Council of Nicea in 325, which declared that the Son was "of the same substance" (*homoousios* in the Greek language of the Council) as the Father. This Council was convened by Emperor Constantine. He was concerned that Arianism was a heresy spreading throughout the empire, threatening political and social stability. Before the influx of Arian Christians into North Africa, Augustine did not have much occasion in his work as a bishop to confront the heresy. After 410, in this homily and in other specifically anti-Arian writings, he does take up the challenge. He is concerned that his people not succumb to what he considered a radical distortion of Christian faith.

2 In this and the following sentences, Augustine is directly confronting Arius's notion that the Word was created by the Father and therefore is not eternal and not divine. He challenges his congregation (there may have been Arian Christians in attendance) to consider that before the creation of the universe there was no time or sequence.

3 Augustine's language here echoes the words of the Nicene Creed about the divinity of Jesus: "God from God, Light from Light, True God from True God."

□ Jesus Christ

The Lord Christ is for ever, without beginning with the Father. And yet ask what today is; it's a birthday.[1] Whose? The Lord's. Has he really got a birthday? He has. The Word in the beginning, God with God, has a birthday? Yes, he has. Unless he had a human birth, we would never attain to the divine rebirth; he was born that we might be reborn. Let nobody hesitate to be reborn; Christ has been born; born, with no need of being reborn. The only ones in need of rebirth are those who have been condemned in their first birth.

And so let his mercy come to be in our hearts. His mother bore him in her womb; let us bear him in our hearts. The virgin was big with the incarnation of Christ; let our bosoms grow big with the faith of Christ. She gave birth to the Savior; let us give birth to praise. We mustn't be barren; our souls must be fruitful with God.

The birth of Christ from the Father was without mother; the birth of Christ from his mother was without father; each birth was wonderful. The first was eternal, the second took place in time.[2] When was he born of the Father? What do you mean, when? You're asking about "when" there, there where you won't find any time? Don't ask about "when" there. Ask about it here; it's a good question, when was he born of his mother. When was he born of the Father is not a good question. He was born, and he has no time; he was born eternal, from the eternal, coeternal.[3] Why be astonished? He's God. Take divinity into consideration, and any reason for astonishment disappears.

And when we say he was born of a virgin, it's a great thing, you're astonished. He's God, don't be astonished; let astonishment give way to thanksgiving and praise. Let faith be present; believe that it happened.

4 A reference to the Eucharist and Holy Communion, which as part of the liturgy would follow shortly after this homily.

5 The incarnation of the Word made flesh climaxes in Christ's Resurrection, in which Christians believe they will share.

6 As we shall see in the next section, Christians believe that the Holy Spirit unites them with Jesus, the Eternal Word, and so with the Holy Trinity. For Augustine, Jesus is both God and the Way to God. Jesus is the pilgrimage route of Christians.

If you don't believe, it still happened, but you remain unbelieving. He agreed to become man; what more do you want? Hasn't God humbled himself enough for you? The one who was God has become man. The inn was crowded and cramped, so he was wrapped in rags, laid in a manger; you heard it when the Gospel was read. Who wouldn't be astonished? The one who filled the universe could find no room in a lodging house; laid in a feeding trough, he became our food.[4]

SERMON 189.3, 4

Christ has made himself a pattern for the life you live now by his labors, his temptations, his sufferings, and his death; and in his resurrection he is the pattern for the life you will live later. Without him, all that we would have known of human life is that we are born and we die; we would not have known that anyone could rise from the dead and live forever.[5] But he took upon himself the human lot you know, and gave you proof of what you did not know. This is why he has become our hope in distress and temptation. Listen to the apostle's encouragement: *We even glory in our sufferings, knowing that suffering fosters endurance, and endurance constancy, and constancy hope; but hope does not disappoint us because the love of God has been poured out into our hearts through the Holy Spirit who has been given us* (Romans 5:3–5). By giving us the Holy Spirit he has become our hope, and also enabled us to march on toward our hope, for if we had no hope we could not keep marching.[6]

EXPOSITIONS OF THE PSALMS 60.4

7 Augustine often calls Jesus *Medicus*, meaning doctor or physician. It is one of his favorite names for Christ, emphasizing the human need for healing grace.

8 Note here Augustine's theology of our absolute need for divine grace, rejecting Pelagius's suggestion that our healing is in some measure a result of human initiative. Augustine is saying that original sin leaves us so wounded that we cannot even get ourselves to the divine clinic; Christ makes house calls.

✎ At the center of Augustine's faith is the mystery of the incarnation, which is the theological word meaning God took on flesh, God became human. As a Christian, he believed that the second person of the Holy Trinity, the Eternal Word of God, entered creation and history in the person of the Jewish rabbi Jesus of Nazareth. For Augustine, the incarnation is the reversal of Adam and Eve's sinful pride in trying to be "like God" (Genesis 3:5). God empties himself of divinity and becomes "like us," joining in all our contingency and fragility. Augustine loved the text of Saint Paul's letter to the Philippians: "Though he was in the form of God, Jesus did not deem equality with God something to be grasped at. Rather he emptied himself, taking the form of a slave, being born in human likeness" (Philippians 2:6–7). This was the divine act of humility, made out of love for us.

If you follow the humble Jesus, you will arrive at the exalted Christ; if in your sickly health and debility you do not spurn the humble one, you will abide in perfect health and strength with the exalted One. What else, after all, was the reason for Christ's humility, but your debility? You were, you see, completely and irremediably in the grip of your debility; and this was the fact that made so great a doctor come to you.[7] After all, if your sickness had even been such that you were able to go to the doctor, your debility could have seemed to be tolerable. But because you were not able to go to him, he came to you.[8] He came teaching humility. Why? Let us see.

It was because pride would not allow us to return to life and had itself made the human heart exalt itself against God and turn away from life; and the soul, being neglected in its healthy condition of the rules of health and salvation, fell into this state of debility.

SERMON 142.2

[icon] Augustine's theology of the Holy Spirit can be summed up in two words: gift and love. Within the life of the One Triune God, the Spirit is the Eternal Love between Father and Son. Since that shared divine love is perfect, infinite, and eternal, it is itself a Divine Person, coequal with Father and Son. With regard to God's relationship with humankind, Augustine teaches that the Spirit is God's gift to us, drawing us into union with Christ, and through Christ with the Eternal God.

[1] This is one of the triadic analogies that Augustine develops in *The Trinity*. The Spirit is the love shared between Father and Son (or between God and the Word, to be less patriarchal). In Book XIII of *Confessions,* Augustine makes many references to the text in Genesis 1:2, which describes the Spirit of God hovering (or dancing, as some scripture scholars would translate the Hebrew) above the cosmic, primeval waters out of which life emerges. God's "super eminent Love" hovers and dances above and throughout the created universe (*Confessions* XIII.7.8).

[2] The Spirit infuses our minds and hearts and draws us into the life of the Eternal God. This is Augustine's astonishing claim: we humans, individually and together, are destined to share in the dynamic, inner life of God. This is the Gift of God.

[3] In this homily on the First Letter of John, we hear Augustine elaborating one of his favorite themes: God is Love. When we love, we have begun to live the very life of God. The Gift that is the Holy Spirit is no more and no less than love, love for each other that binds us ever more closely to the Love that is God. In the end, Augustine's theology of God is simple and profound: God is Love. When we love each other (and by "we" Augustine would mean any human being who truly loves), we live and move and have our being in the Love of God. The Spirit of God *is* the act of love, according to Peter Lombard, one of the very early commentators on Augustine's theology.

☐ The Holy Spirit

Now love means someone loving and something loved with love. There you are with three: the lover, what is being loved, and love. And what is love but a kind of life coupling or trying to couple together two things, namely lover and what is being loved?[1]

THE TRINITY VIII.5.14

So the love that is from God and is God is distinctively the Holy Spirit; through him the charity of God is poured out in our hearts, and through it the whole triad dwells in us.[2] This is the reason why it is most apposite that the Holy Spirit, while being God, should also be called the Gift of God. And this Gift, surely, is distinctively to be understood as being the charity that brings us through to God, without which no other Gift of God at all can bring us through to God.

THE TRINITY XV.5.32

No one has ever seen God (1 John 4:12). See, beloved: *If we love one another, God will abide in us, and God's love will be perfected in us* (4:12). Begin to love, to be made perfect. Have you begun to love? God has begun to dwell in you.[3] Love God who has begun to dwell in you, so that by dwelling in you more perfectly, God may make you perfect. *We know that we abide in God, and God in us, because God has given us of the Spirit* (4:13). Good! Thanks be to God! We know that God dwells in us. And how do we know this very thing, that we have known that God dwells in us? Because John himself said, *Because God has given us of the Spirit.* How do we know that *God has given us of the Spirit?* How do *you* know this very thing, that God has given *you* of the Spirit? Ask your heart. If it is filled with charity, you have God's Spirit. How do we know that that is how you know that

4 We all know how difficult it can be at times to love others, even those we cherish deeply. As Augustine would put it, the pride, arrogance, and self-centeredness that afflict us because of original sin impede our will to love. The Gift of the Holy Spirit overcomes sin by attracting us to the good works of love, by impelling us toward the humility, compassion, and altruism that comprise acts of love (yet, as we have seen in the section on Pelagianism, all the while respecting our free will). Augustine believes it is through the Holy Spirit that divine grace fills our minds and hearts, calling us to acts of love by revealing what is the loving thing to do, and by attracting us to act accordingly.

5 Augustine is commenting on the Gift of the Holy Spirit, which is understood by Christians to be bestowed through the sacrament of baptism—a "visible sign" of the Spirit. But what about people who lived before Jesus and who could not have received Christian baptism? Sacred scripture describes King David, Elizabeth (the mother of John the Baptist), Anna and Simeon (mentioned in the Gospel of Luke), and others as "filled with the Holy Spirit."

6 Augustine directly answers this question about the Spirit of God dwelling in persons beyond the Christian community of the baptized. God's providence is not limited by historical accidents of time or space. The indwelling of God's own Spirit in human beings is "ineffable and incomprehensible" and no one person's or one religion's prerogative.

God's Spirit dwells in you? Ask the apostle Paul: *Because the charity of God has been poured out in our hearts through the Holy Spirit, who has been given to us* (Romans 5:5).

HOMILIES ON THE FIRST EPISTLE OF JOHN 8.12

God bestows love by the Holy Spirit so that the delight of sin may be conquered by the delight of that love.[4]

UNFINISHED WORK IN ANSWER TO JULIAN 1.107

For if the Holy Spirit was not in human beings before the Lord's visible glorification, how could David say, *Do not remove your Holy Spirit from me* (Psalm 51:11)? Or how could Elizabeth and her husband Zechariah be filled so that they could prophesy, and also Anna and Simeon, concerning all of who it is written that they were filled with the Holy Spirit and spoke those things which we read in the Gospel?[5] But that God does some things in a hidden way but others in a visible way by means of a visible creature is a matter of the governance of providence, by which all divine actions are accomplished with order and with the most splendid refinement in regard to times and places, inasmuch as divinity itself is neither confined to a place nor changes place, nor does it bend or fluctuate with respect to time....[6] We have said this so that we may understand that by the visible appearance of the Holy Spirit, which is called his coming, his fullness has been poured more abundantly into the hearts of human beings in an ineffable and incomprehensible way.

MISCELLANY OF EIGHTY-THREE QUESTIONS 63

[7] This short sentence summarizes the whole previous annotation. In Augustine's understanding of God, the Spirit infuses our will so that we are drawn to the good and right thing to do for the sake of love. If we choose to act, we are filled with the peace of God that follows upon the act of love. In the rest of this famous passage from *Confessions*, Augustine elaborates the analogy of things being drawn toward their proper object or goal, their "weight" (*pondus* in Latin).

[8] Our weight, our "rightful place," is love. God's Gift of the Spirit draws us to loving.

Our true place is where we find rest. We are borne toward it by love, and it is your good Spirit who lifts up our sunken nature from the gates of death. In goodness of will is our peace.[7] A body gravitates to its proper place by its own weight. This weight does not necessarily drag it downward, but pulls it to the place proper to it: thus fire tends upward, a stone downward. Drawn by their weight, things seek their rightful places. If oil is poured into water, it will rise to the surface, but if water is poured onto oil, it will sink below the oil: drawn by their weight, things seek their rightful places.[8] They are not at rest as long as they are disordered, but once brought to order, they find their rest. Now, my weight is my love, and wherever I am carried, it is this weight that carries me. Your Gift sets us afire and we are borne upward; we catch his flame and up we go. In our hearts we climb those upward paths, singing the songs of ascent (see Psalms 119–133).

CONFESSIONS XIII.9.10

In the Gospels, Christ gives his command to love one another and to love one's enemy. Augustine relates and roots his teaching about this command in his theology of the Holy Spirit. Human love and divine love are distinguished not by a difference of substance, but a difference of degree. Every act of love by every human being is a participation in the divine reality. As Augustine sees it, we humans struggle to love because of sin. But God's grace, given to us through the Spirit that suffuses all creation, gradually perfects our ability to love by drawing our wills to acts of love. Gradually, as we grow in our ability to love, we become more and more like God.

1 Augustine uses two words for love: *caritas*, which is usually translated as "charity," and *amor*, which is usually translated as "love." He comments that both have the same meaning, and the human reality that they name is a revelatory act of God.

2 For Augustine, our acts of love, inspired and empowered by God's Holy Spirit, are in themselves continuing acts of divine creation. Our acts of love change the world, transforming enemies into friends. To express it in the language of the New Testament, our acts of love help inaugurate God's kingdom on earth.

☐ Loving One Another

You see now with faith; then you will see by appearance. For, if we love when we don't see, how we shall embrace when we do see! But where must we practice? By loving one another! You can tell me, "I haven't seen God." Can you tell me, "I haven't seen a human being"? Love one another. For, if you love the one whom you see, you will see God at the same time, because you will see charity itself, and God dwells within it.[1]

HOMILIES ON THE FIRST EPISTLE OF JOHN 5.7

And if someone is full of love, what is he or she full of but God?

THE TRINITY VIII.5.12

Ask God that you may love one another. You should love all people, even your enemies, not because they are your brother or sister, but so that they may become your brother or sister, so that you may always be aflame with such love, whether toward one who has become your brother or sister, or toward your enemies, so that by loving them they may become your brothers and sisters.[2]

HOMILIES ON THE FIRST EPISTLE OF JOHN 10.7

3   This passage, written early in Augustine's ministry as bishop, recalls the importance of his theme of the ordering of love that we explored in Part Two (pages 40–42). Love is not just affection. It is active engagement for the benefit of another, in light of God's love for their well-being. Thus love needs to be thoughtful, ethically judicious, and morally discriminating for the benefit of those entrusted to us by God through the "accident" of our personal history.

Living a just and holy life requires one to be capable of an objective and impartial evaluation of things;[3] to love things, that is to say, in the right order, so that you do not love what is not to be loved, or fail to love what is to be loved, or have a greater love for what should be loved less, or an equal love for things that should be loved less or more, or a lesser or greater love for things that should be loved equally. No sinner, precisely as a sinner, is to be loved; and every human being, precisely as a human, is to be loved on God's account, God though on his own. And if God is to be loved more than any human being, we all ought to love God more than ourselves....

All people are to be loved equally; but since you cannot be of service to everyone, you have to take greater care of those who are more closely joined to you by a turn, so to say, of fortune's wheel, whether by occasion of place or time, or any other such circumstance.

On Christian Instruction 1.27.28; 28.29

➤ Augustine's many passages on friendship are among the most moving of his writings. His *Confessions* as well as his many letters reveal how much friendship meant to him, and how throughout his life he was surrounded by family and friends. Even when he became bishop, he wanted to live in a monastic community, together with those who shared in his faith and his ministry.

Augustine believed friendship to be a particular expression of love, and so a particular revelation of God's love and of the life of the Holy Spirit.

1 This passage is one of "eighty-three responses" written over the years to answer occasional questions asked of Augustine by his fellow monks at Thagaste and then at Hippo.

2 For example, it must have been difficult for the young Augustine to make new, authentic friends as he rose to the top of the hierarchy in the Roman imperial court. Likewise, when he later rose from being a monk to being a leading bishop in the Catholic Church, laypeople and even his fellow monks may have been put off by his status and reputation.

☐ Friendship

The friendship of no one who seeks to become our friend should be rejected—not that he should be received at once [into our friendship] but that we should be open to receiving him and to treating him in such a way that he can be received.[1] For we can say that a person has been received into our friendship when we dare to disclose all our thoughts to him. And if there is anyone who does not dare to make friends with us because he is embarrassed on account of some temporal honor or dignity of ours, we should approach him on his own level and offer him with a certain courtesy and humility of soul what he dares not ask for of himself.[2]

It sometimes happens, to be sure, although it is rather rare, that the bad qualities of a person whom we wish to receive into our friendship become known to us before his good ones do, that we are offended and to a certain extent repelled by them, and that we leave him and never find out his good qualities, which are perhaps concealed. And so the Lord Jesus Christ, who wishes us to become his imitators, admonishes us to tolerate the person's weakness, so that we may be led by way of a charitable tolerance to those healthy qualities whose enjoyment would give us pleasure....

But often good qualities are the first to appear. A rash but kindly judgment in their regard should be cautioned against as well, lest, having thought of someone as totally good, the bad qualities that appear later come upon you when you are settled and unprepared and they offend you all the more, so that you hate more passionately the person whom you had so rashly loved, which is wicked. For even if no good qualities were evident to begin with, and those that first stood out

3 In other words, remember that no friend is ever perfect, despite a natural tendency to idealize new friends.

4 This sentence and the next paragraph come from a long letter written by Augustine around the year 411 to a wealthy Roman widow named Proba. She was one of the exiles fleeing Rome because of Alaric's invasion of the city in 410. Proba had written to Augustine about the nature of prayer. Augustine's letter to her is a reflection on how and for what we should pray. One of the gifts we should pray for, Augustine writes, is friendship. That counsel must have been particularly poignant for Proba, whose exile from Italy no doubt separated her from many lifelong friends.

5 There is a radical humanism in Augustine, based on his belief that all human beings are made in God's image, for God's love, and potentially filled with God's Spirit. In today's world, Augustine would certainly consider himself a citizen of the world, interested in and respectful of persons from every culture and religion. The following selection is in the same vein.

were those that would later prove to be bad, they should still be tolerated until you had done everything in his regard that usually contributes to healing in such cases. How much more should this be the case when those good qualities have come first that serve as pledges and that ought to constrain us to tolerate the later ones.

This, then, is the law of Christ—that we should bear one another's burdens.[3]

MISCELLANY OF EIGHTY-THREE QUESTIONS 71.6

Without a friend, nothing in the world seems friendly.[4]

LETTER 130.2.4

Friendship should not be bounded by narrow limits, for it embraces all to whom we owe affection and love, though it is inclined more eagerly toward some and more hesitantly toward others. It, however, extends even to enemies, for whom we are also commanded to pray. Thus, there is no one in the human race to whom we do not owe love, even if not out of mutual love, at least on account of our sharing in a common nature.[5]

LETTER 130.13

Friendship begins with married partner and children, and from there moves on to strangers. But if we consider that we all have one father and one mother [Adam and Eve], who will be a stranger? Every human being is neighbor to every other human being. Ask nature; is he unknown? He's human. Is she an enemy? She's human. Is he a foe? He's human. Is she a friend? Let her stay a friend. Is he an enemy? Let him become a friend.

SERMON 299D.1

6 This passage is from a letter to Saint Jerome whom Augustine never met in person. Jerome had lived in Rome, before moving to Bethlehem. They were friends by correspondence over many years. Jerome could be quite critical of Augustine—and of many others as well. (He's known for being the most disagreeable father of the church.) Augustine was deferential, but on occasion disagreed with Jerome over theological matters and scriptural interpretations and translations. Their friendship was all through correspondence, but valued nonetheless by Augustine.

I by no means think that you could have become angry unless I either said what I ought not to have or did not say it as I ought to have, for I am not surprised that we know each other less well than we are known by our closest and most intimate friends. I admit that I find it easy to abandon my whole self to the love of them, especially when I am wearied by the scandals of the world, and I find rest in that love without any worry. I, of course, feel that God is in that person to whom I abandon myself with security and in whom I find rest in security. And in that security I do not at all fear that incertitude of tomorrow stemming from human fragility....**6**

LETTER 73.10

Is it not a common experience that when we show certain lovely vistas to a dear friend for the first time, our own delight is renewed by their delight at the novelty of the scene? Our reawakened joy is heightened by the passion of our friendship. It seems that the more we love our friends, the more old things become new for us.

INSTRUCTING BEGINNERS IN THE FAITH 12.17

There were other joys to be found in their company, which still more powerfully captivated my mind—the charms of talking and laughing together and kindly giving way to each other's wishes, reading elegantly written books together, sharing jokes and delighting to honor one another, disagreeing occasionally but without rancor, as a person might disagree with himself, and lending piquancy by that rare disagreement to our much more frequent accord. We would teach and learn from each other, sadly missing all who were absent and blithely welcoming them when they returned. Such signs of friendship sprang from the hearts of friends who love and know their love returned, signs to be read in smiles, words, glances, and a thousand other gracious gestures. So were sparks kindled and our minds were fused inseparably, out of many becoming one.

7 | This beautifully written passage occurs in *Confessions* just after Augustine tells us about the death of a childhood friend who passed away suddenly when both Augustine and he were young adults, about twenty-one years of age, living in Thagaste. The death devastated Augustine, particularly because his friend had just rejected Augustine's Manichean proselytizing a day or so before he died. Augustine was so distraught that he left his hometown and returned to Carthage to teach there.

Friendship was one of the ways through which Augustine's grief slowly healed. This passage refers immediately to his friends in Carthage, among the students and faculty there. But the bishop, who wrote these lines twenty or so years later, allows his poetic prose to rise above the particular painful memory he is recalling to describe the gift of the many good friends whom he treasured throughout his life.

This is what we esteem in our friends, and so highly do we esteem it that our conscience feels guilt if we fail to love someone who responds to us with love, or do not return the love of one who offers love to us, and this without seeking any bodily gratification from the other save signs of his goodwill.[7]

CONFESSIONS IV.8.13, 14

⟦◥⟧ As Augustine writes so often, God is love, and our growth in loving is the Gift of God's Spirit. He understands friendship to be a special kind of love and community to be an association of friends gathered together with a common purpose. For Augustine, God is discovered in the experience of community.

Augustine's first experiment with Christian community was the four- or five-month retreat that he made with his mother, his brother, his son, and several friends and students at Cassiciacum before his baptism. He writes in *Confessions* about his desire and his plans to live in community with likeminded friends (VI.14.24). In 388, a year or so after his baptism, he returned to his hometown in Africa to establish such a community. That lasted only a few years, because in 391 he was called to be ordained for service to the Church of Hippo.

As priest and then bishop, Augustine's immediate experience of community was the family of monks that lived with him in Hippo. Then there was the wider community of his associates and friends in Hippo, and the neighboring churches in other North African cities and across the Mediterranean. As we shall see, the church for Augustine is at its essence a community of believers united by God's Holy Spirit.

1 It is helpful to state once again that *Letter* 130 was written to Proba and her family who had just been exiled from their home in Rome. The friendship experienced in and through community helps us get through life's troubles.

2 This description of stags is found in Pliny's natural history—Augustine liked this example and used it also in his *Expositions of the Psalms* 41 and 129.

3 This is another response by Augustine to the eighty-three questions put to him over many years by his brother monks. Question 71 was a request for his comments on Galatians 6:2: *Bear one another's burdens, and thus you will fulfill the law of Christ.*

☐ Community

Good human beings seem even in this life to provide no small consolation. For, if poverty pinches, if grief saddens, if bodily pain disturbs, if exile discourages, if any other disaster torments, provided that there are present good human beings who know not only how *to rejoice with those in joy*, but also *to weep with those who weep* (Romans 12:15) and can speak and converse in a helpful way, those rough spots are smoothed, the heavy burdens are lightened, and adversity is overcome.[1]

LETTER 130.2.4

Now, while we are in this life, which is to say on this journey, let us bear one another's burdens, so that we may be able to attain to that life in which there are no burdens at all. Some learned persons[2] who possess knowledge of this sort have written this about stags: When they cross over a body of water to an island in order to feed, they arrange themselves so as to put the burden of their heads, which are heavy with antlers, upon each other in such a way that the one behind stretches his neck and places his head on the one before him. And since there has to be one who leads the rest and has no one in front of him to lay his head on, they are said to take turns, so that the one who is in the lead and is worn out by the burden of his head goes to the end of the line, and the one whose head he bore when he himself was first, takes his place. Bearing one another's burdens in this fashion, they cross over the water until they come to solid ground.... Nothing so proves a friend as bearing a friend's burden.[3]

MISCELLANY OF EIGHTY-THREE QUESTIONS 71.1

4 Augustine wrote a rule of life to guide those who wished to live in community. There are several versions of his monastic rule, written at different times and in different circumstances for communities of monks and nuns. These variant texts soon came together to be known as the Rule of Saint Augustine. It is the oldest monastic rule in the Western or Latin Church, written one hundred and twenty years before the Rule of Saint Benedict, and eight hundred years before the Rule of Saint Francis of Assisi.

Augustine's rule focuses on the common good by emphasizing that all things are to be held in common, and that members of the community should look out for each other. Unlike the Rule of Saint Benedict, Augustine's does not provide a strict and detailed monastic schedule, but rather allows for the flexibility that service to the wider community might demand or local circumstance require. For sixteen hundred years, Augustine's rule of life has guided monastic and mendicant communities in the church, such as the Augustinian Friars and Nuns, the Norbertines, the Dominicans, the Servites, and many other communities of religious sisters and brothers.

5 Possidius was one of Augustine's brother monks and a longtime friend, and eventually himself a bishop. Shortly after Augustine's death, Possidius wrote a brief life of Augustine, the first such biography of the bishop of Hippo. This work is charming in its simplicity and straightforward in its presentation. It also provides many insights into Augustine's daily life in the monastery and in the ministry. Possidius also supplied a list of Augustine's writings at the end of his biography.

6 This interesting detail reminds us that monastic life is no paradise. Original sin works its way into religious communities as well as into any other. In one letter, Augustine himself remarks that in the monastery he "met the best of men and the worst of men" (*Letter* 78.9).

Before all else, beloved, love God and then your neighbor, for these are the chief commandments given to us. The following are the precepts we order you living in the monastery to observe. The main purpose for your having come together is to live harmoniously in your house, intent upon God with one heart and one soul. Therefore, call nothing your own, but let everything be yours in common. Food and clothing shall be distributed to each of you by your superior, not equally to all, for all do not enjoy equal health, but rather according to each one's need. For so you read in the Acts of the Apostles that "they had all things in common, and each was given what he needed" (Acts 4:32,35).**4**

MONASTIC RULE I.1–4

From the first biography written about Augustine:

His meals were frugal and economical; at times, however, in addition to herbs and vegetables they included meat for the sake of guests or sick brethren. Moreover, they always included wine, for he knew and taught, with the apostle, that *everything created by God is good, and nothing is to be rejected if it is received with thanksgiving; for then it is consecrated by the Word of God and prayer* (1 Timothy 4:4–5)....

He practiced hospitality at all times. Even at table he found more delight in reading and conversation than in eating and drinking.**5**

To prevent one plague that afflicts social intercourse, he had these words inscribed on the table: "Let those who lie to slander the lives of the absent know that their own are not worthy of this table." In this way, he reminded all his guests that they ought to abstain from unnecessary and harmful gossip.**6**

THE LIFE OF SAINT AUGUSTINE BY SAINT POSSIDIUS XXII.2, 6

When Augustine was baptized at the age of thirty-one in 387 by Bishop Ambrose in Milan, he became a full member of the Catholic Church. The Catholic Church was familiar to him from his childhood. His mother's faithful practice of Catholicism and his own attendance at liturgical services over the years as a casual observer meant that the church was a definite if distant part of his life experience. Throughout his youth and young adulthood, he explored other religious and philosophical systems, until his conversion and baptism.

By 388, Augustine was back in Africa, intending to live a Christian community life of prayer and study with likeminded friends at his family home in Thagaste. Within three years, however, he was called to the priesthood while on a visit to Hippo. By 395, he was bishop. So in a period of five years, Augustine went from someone on the fringes of the church to an ordained leader of the church.

In a way typical of his keen mind, Augustine reflected on the purpose of this community of believers he had joined and was now leading. He developed an "ecclesiology," or a theology of church, exploring the deeper meanings and spiritual connections that united the community of believers. Augustine taught that through baptism and the Gift of the Holy Spirit, a believer is united with Jesus Christ, a "member" of Christ's body, an extension of the mystery of the Word made flesh through history. This was the essence of church for Augustine, as he understood it through the writings of the New Testament, especially the letters of Saint Paul.

1 This phrase, the "whole Christ" (*totus Christus* in Latin), is an important, recurring theme in Augustine's understanding of the church. The mystery of the incarnation, of the Eternal Word made flesh, did not end with the life and death of Jesus of Nazareth. The Holy Spirit unites each believer with the mystery of Christ. Through that communion with Christ, the baptized Christian continues Jesus's mission and message, and together with all other believers is Christ's real presence throughout time and space. This is Augustine's elaboration of Saint Paul's notion of the body of Christ (Ephesians 4) and what is known in Catholic teaching as "the Mystical Body of Christ."

☐ The Church

When Christ has begun to dwell in our inmost being through faith, when we have confessed and invoked him, and he has begun to take possession of us, then is formed the whole Christ, head and body, one from the many.[1] From now on listen to the words of Christ.... Let us listen to this speaker, and in him speak as ourselves. Let us be his members, so that this voice may be ours as well.... So Christ is preaching himself, telling the good news of himself even through his members, those who already belong to him. Through them he can attract others, who will be joined to the members through whom his Gospel has been spread. One body is to be formed, under one head, living one life in one Spirit.

EXPOSITIONS OF THE PSALMS 74.4

2   Note how in this homily Augustine roots the reality of the church as the body of Christ in the practice of love.

3   This idea of amputation or separation from the church needs explanation. Augustine also used Saint Paul's image of cutting off branches from the vine—and of grafting new branches onto that same vine (see Romans 11). The church as the body of Christ is a dynamic, living reality, not just a juridical authority. Once baptized into the body of Christ, a person can separate from that community of faith by his or her own decision. For Augustine, such separation is significant: hence the images of amputation or cutting. And in his theology, there was no help for those who had separated themselves from Christ. (*Extra ecclesiam nulla salus*—"outside the church, no salvation"—was the way his predecessor, Bishop Cyprian of Carthage, had expressed it a century earlier.) So willfully leaving the church was a serious matter for Augustine, for it implied rejection of the Eternal Word made flesh.

4   This paragraph presents another aspect of Augustine's understanding of the church. There is the church in this world, subject to the vicissitudes of history, and the church in heaven, of those united with Christ through baptism who have already passed on to enjoy eternal union with God. The two are united in what is called in the Christian Creed the "communion of saints."

5   This idea of the universal church was important for Augustine. The church as "Catholic" means universal, from the Greek *katholikos* ("concerning the whole"). For Augustine, the mystery of each baptized believer's union with Christ, and through Christ with all other believers, transcends any accidents of time, place, culture, language, custom, or history.

Today's distinction between Catholic and Protestant derives from the Reformation movements of the sixteenth and seventeenth centuries. In Augustine's day, the word "Catholic" distinguished congregations from the Donatists, or from the Arians and other heretical movements.

Your faith, dearly beloved, is not unaware—and I know that this is what you have learned from the teaching of the Master in heaven, in whom you have placed your hope—that our Lord Jesus Christ, who has already suffered and risen again for us, is the head of the church; and that the church is his body, and that in his body, as its very health, is to be found the unity of its members and the framework of love. Anyone who grows cold in love is sick in the body of Christ.[2]

But God, who has already raised our head on high, has the power to heal the sick members too, provided, that is, that they haven't amputated themselves by extreme wickedness, but stick in the body until they are healed. Whatever, you see, remains in the body need not despair of being restored to health; but any part that has been amputated can be neither treated nor healed.[3]

Since then he is the head of the church, and the church is his body, the whole Christ is both head and body.

Sermon 137.1

God himself lives in Zion, which means "watching," and bears the image of the church that now is, as Jerusalem bears the image of the church that is yet to be, that is, of the city of the saints who enjoy the angelic life. This is because Jerusalem means "vision of peace." Watching goes before seeing, as this church precedes that other church which is promised, the immortal and eternal city.[4]

Expositions of the Psalms 9.12

The holy church is what we are; but I don't mean "we" in the sense of just those of us who are here, you that are listening to me now; as many of us as are here by the grace of God Christian believers in this church, that is in this city, as many as there are in this region, as many as there are in this province, as many as there are also across the sea, as many as there are in the whole wide world, since *from the rising of the sun to its setting the name of the Lord is praised* (Psalm 113:3). Such is the Catholic Church, our true mother, the true consort of that bridegroom.[5]

Sermon 213.8

6 By "enemies," Augustine could be referring to the pagans, Donatists, Arians, Manicheans, Jews, former Catholics—anyone who was not a member of the Catholic Church he led, and many who were on the other side of his often-searing theological arguments. His point in this important paragraph, which comes at the beginning of his monumental work *City of God,* is that it is not our place to judge others, nor to put them in set categories that define them according to our purposes. The church is made of saints and sinners. And the world, that is, those political, social, and religious realities outside the church, is also made of saints and sinners. As he puts it in a homily about his own church: "How many sheep there are without, how many wolves within!" (*Homilies on the Gospel of John* 45.12).

7 Hypocritical Christians.

8 One of the main lessons we can draw from this first book in the *City of God* is that the ecclesial and social categories within which we make our lives are important, but not definitive. The deeper mysteries of divine grace and the actions of God's Spirit within the souls of human beings are what Augustine considers more important and more inscrutable. Hence, his abiding advice is to refrain from judging others and forcing them into neat categories. To borrow from the Gospel parable Augustine used: wheat and weeds are growing up side by side in the church, and by extension of Augustine's argument outside the church as well. Only at final judgment will there be a final separation and revelation of good and evil (*City of God* XX.9.1).

This is indeed good advice in today's intercultural world where religions mix and intermingle on a daily basis, and where judgmental attitudes can lead to intolerance and violence. In Augustine's understanding of church, there is no room for triumphalism, intolerance, and sanctimonious self-righteousness. His readiness to provide strongly reasoned arguments for his beliefs should not be confused with a lack of respect for his theological adversaries. In a homily preached on the anniversary of his ordination, he challenges those with whom he has engaged in heated debate: "Pay me back love for love!" (*Sermon* 383.2).

The church must bear in mind that among its "enemies" are hidden her future citizens; and when confronted with them, she must not think it fruitless to tolerate their hostility until she finds them confessing the faith.[6] In the same way, while the City of God is on pilgrimage in this world, the church has some members who participate in the unity of the sacraments, but who will not share with her in the eternal destiny of the saints. Some of these members are hidden; some are well known— the ones who do not hesitate to complain against God, whose sacramental sign they bear, even as they mingle with acknowledged enemies. Sometimes they join with God's enemies attending the theaters, at other times they join with us attending our churches.[7]

But such as they are, we have less right to despair that they might reform, when some predestined friends, unknown as yet even to themselves, are hidden among our most open enemies. In truth, those two cities are interwoven and intermixed in this era and await separation at the last judgment.[8]

CITY OF GOD I.35

9 In this letter, written between 406 and 412, Augustine is answering several questions posed to him by a priest. One of the priest's questions concerns all those people who lived well before the time of Jesus, both pagans and Jews. Were they outside the possibility of salvation? In his response, Augustine expands his understanding of church. As a Christian, Augustine believes that Jesus, who is God come among us, is the only way to God. However, he suggests that any religion that helps its adherents lead good lives actually puts them in touch with the reality of the Word of God among us.

10 Augustine presumes that the Jewish people were expecting the Messiah to be God "in the flesh," as Christians believe. That is not an accurate, or at least not the only, interpretation of Jewish Messianic expectations. Nonetheless, Augustine identifies strong continuity between Jews and Christians—an unusual argument for his time. This continuity of faith led Augustine to be protective of the Jewish communities of his day, as contemporary scholar Paula Fredrickson argues.

11 Once again we hear Augustine counseling tolerance among religions and respect for those who are different with regard to faith and worship. The same God is calling out to all of us. This is a very different approach from the very exclusive understanding of church taught by the Donatist Christians of North Africa.

All those from the beginning of the human race who believed in him and understood him somehow or other and lived pious and just lives according to those commandments, whenever and wherever they lived, were undoubtedly saved through him.[9] For, just as we believe in him as both remaining with the Father and as having come in the flesh, so the people of old believed in him as remaining with the Father and as going to come in the flesh.[10] The faith itself has not changed, nor is salvation itself different, because in accord with the different times there is now proclaimed as already having happened what was then foretold as coming. Nor do we need to think that the realities are different or that the means of salvation are different because one and the same reality is either predicted or proclaimed with different ceremonies and sacraments. Regarding which events should happen at what time from among those events pertaining to one and the same deliverance of the faithful and pious, let us leave the plan to God; let us hold onto obedience for ourselves.[11]

LETTER 102.12

◥ There is a distinction in theology between heresy and schism. Heresy refers to a group or sect that teaches something fundamentally different from what the church considers orthodox or correct. So, for example, the Arians, who taught that Jesus was not the Son of God—clearly different from what the majority of Christians believed—were called heretics.

A schism is a split within the church over some practice or discipline. The Donatists were schismatic because, although they taught basic Christian doctrine and practiced the same sacraments, they insisted on rebaptizing anyone who had been baptized by a wayward cleric. Augustine, as we have seen in the Introduction, had to confront this schism that was tearing the North African church apart.

1 Augustine wrote this letter when he was still a priest in the early 390s to the Donatist bishop Maximinus in Siniti, Numidia. Augustine is trying to determine if Maximinus rebaptized a Catholic deacon and begs him not to do so if he hasn't already.

2 Even early in his priesthood, long before he became the chief spokesperson of the Catholics against the Donatists, Augustine tried to separate theological argument from social and political forces, and to appeal to the Donatists in a fraternal context free of any coercion. We know that in this case it worked. Maximinus sometime later left the Donatist Church and continued his ministry as a Catholic bishop.

3 This sentence summarizes the situation of physical violence that came to characterize the conflict. The Circumcellions were particularly ferocious. They were rural, terrorist cells, organized to attack Catholics by blinding, maiming, and killing laity and clergy. When attacking luckless travelers who wandered into their ambushes, they would shout out their rallying cry: *"Deus Magnus"*—"God is Great."

□ The Donatists

Though I express in the strongest words I can my hatred for the lamentable and deplorable custom of people in this region who, though they boast of the Christian name, do not hesitate to rebaptize Christians, there were some people who praised you and who said to me that you do not do that....[1] To rebaptize, then, a heretical person who has already received these signs of holiness that the Christian discipline has handed down is a sin without a doubt. To rebaptize a Catholic is, however, a most grievous sin. And yet, not believing this report since I held a good opinion of you, I myself went to Mutugenna, and I could not see the poor man, but I heard from his parents that he has now also become your deacon. And I still think so well of your disposition of heart that I do not believe that he was baptized again.

Hence, I beg you, most dear brother, by the divinity and the humanity of our Lord Jesus Christ, to be so good as to write back to me what has happened and to write back in such a way that you bear in mind that I want to read your letter to our brothers in the church.... And I will not do this when the army is present for fear that someone of yours might think that I wanted to do this with more violence than the cause of peace requires.[2] I will do it after the departure of the army in order that all who hear us may understand that it is not part of my purpose that people be forced against their will into communion with anyone, but that the truth may become known to those who seek it most peacefully. Terror from temporal authorities will cease on our side; let there also cease on your side terror from bands of Circumcellions.[3]

LETTER 23.2, 3, 7

4 This long letter—Augustine actually called it a book—was written to a man named Boniface who was tribune and then count of Africa. He explains the nature and history of the Donatist controversy to Boniface, who was unfamiliar with it, but who had responsibility for enforcing the laws against the Donatists. Augustine's position is to try every reasonable way to bring the Donatists into union with the Catholics before resorting to legal enforcement that involved physical coercion.

5 The original position of Catholic bishops was to request laws that protected them against Donatist violence and allowed them to practice their faith in peace.

6 Augustine himself had been the target of the Circumcellions as he was traveling back to Hippo from a pastoral trip. An unintended change of route spared his life.

Before these laws by which they are being forced to come into the holy banquet were promulgated in Africa, some brothers, among whom I was included, thought that, though the madness of the Donatists was raging everywhere, we should not ask the emperors to give order that this heresy be completely eliminated by establishing a punishment for those who chose to remain in it.[4] Rather, we thought that we should ask that they establish laws so that those who preach the Catholic truth by speaking it or who read the scriptures to determine it should not suffer the Donatists' insane acts of violence. We thought that this could be achieved in some measure if they reaffirmed more explicitly against the Donatists, who denied that they were heretics, the law of Theodosius of most pious memory, which he promulgated against all the heresies in general, namely, "That any bishop or cleric of theirs, wherever he is found, should be fined ten pounds of gold." We did not want all of them to be fined in that way but only those in whose territories the Catholic Church suffered some acts of violence from their clerics, from the Circumcellions, or from their people, so that, following a complaint from the Catholics who had suffered such violence, their bishops or other ministers would be held to the payment of the fine by the care of those in charge. For we thought that, if they were thoroughly frightened and did not dare to do anything of the sort, we could freely teach and hold the Catholic truth....[5]

LETTER 185.7.25

I lost my way at a crossroads and so did not pass through a place where I would have been ambushed by an armed band of Donatists had they discovered me traveling there, and so it happened that I arrived at my destination by a circuitous route, and when I discovered they had laid an ambush I was glad that I had lost my way and gave thanks for this to God.[6]

THE ENCHIRIDION OF FAITH, HOPE, AND CHARITY 5.17

7 Even when he invokes Roman law against the Donatists, Augustine always argues against physical torture and capital punishment. He prefers that civil fines and, if necessary, imprisonment be used to deter acts of physical violence and reduce social tension so that reasoned argument could prevail and persuade. It is interesting that Augustine, considered a pessimist regarding human nature because of his teaching about original sin, always held out hope that even terrorists could change if grace were given a chance to influence them.

The wild mobs of the Donatists made it necessary to do what was done on account of them for they did not know what had been previously settled, and it had to be shown to them.

UNFINISHED WORK IN ANSWER TO JULIAN I.10

Would anyone doubt that it is better to bring human beings to worship God by instruction than by the fear or the pain of punishment? But, because the former are better, it does not mean that the latter, who are not such, should be neglected. For it has benefited many, as we have found and continue to find by experience, to be first forced by fear or pain so that later they may be instructed or may put into practice what they have already learned verbally.[7]

LETTER 185.6.21

1 Augustine explains that though there are many different signs and symbols in the Hebrew Bible, as well as in the Christian Church, certain ones have a preeminence for Christian believers. These central symbols are what the church comes to call its sacraments.

2 Augustine stresses the importance of understanding the meaning of the sacramental signs, and of celebrating them with awareness and insight. He rejects any kind of ritualism or mechanical performance of rites without informed and assenting faith. His reference to "carnal rites" is a rather dismissive attitude toward Jewish rituals such as Passover, the sacrifices of the Second Temple worship in Jesus's time, and other purification rites, which he believes have been superseded by Christian sacraments.

3 Augustine preached this homily on Easter Sunday morning to those who were newly baptized during the Easter vigil the night before. On Easter Sunday and during the weeks following Easter, the newly baptized were taught the meaning of the sacraments they received. In this homily, he explains the sacraments of baptism, the anointing with oil (which would later separate in the Western Church from baptism and become known as confirmation), and Eucharist or Holy Communion. He goes on in this sermon to explain parts of the Mass or eucharistic celebration.

4 A reference to what Catholics believe is the "real presence" of Christ under the forms of bread and wine during the eucharistic celebration. Various theologies or attempts to understand this teaching arise in the Middle Ages and during the Protestant Reformation.

5 This is a favorite theme of Augustine. Christians, in receiving the eucharistic bread and wine become what they see, that is, the presence of Christ in the world. This has been called "divinization" in Augustine's theology. It is not just the bread and wine that is transformed, but those who receive it also become the body and blood of Christ. This is the purpose and the mystery of the sacrament.

☐ The Sacraments

The Lord himself and the discipline of the apostles have handed down to us just a few signs instead of many, and these so easy to perform, and so awesome to understand, and so pure and chaste to celebrate, such as the sacrament of baptism, and the celebration of the Lord's body and blood.[1] When people receive these, they have been so instructed that they can recognize to what sublime realities they are to be referred, and so they venerate them in a spirit not of carnal slavery, but rather of spiritual freedom.[2]

TEACHING CHRISTIANITY III.9.13

I had promised those of you who have just been baptized a sermon to explain the sacrament of the Lord's table, which you can see right now, and which you shared in last night.[3] You ought to know what you have received, what you are about to receive, what you ought to receive every day. That bread that you can see on the altar, sanctified by the Word of God, is the body of Christ. That cup, or rather what the cup contains, sanctified by the Word of God, is the blood of Christ.[4] It was by means of these things that the Lord Christ wished to present us with his body and blood, which he shed for our sake for the forgiveness of sins. If you receive them well, you are yourselves what you receive.[5] You see, the apostle says, *We, being many, are one loaf, one body* (1 Corinthians 10:17). That's how he explained the sacrament of the Lord's table; one loaf, one body, is what we all are, many though we be.

6 He refers to the Lenten observance of prayer and fasting, prior to baptism at the Easter vigil service. At various services during the weeks of Lent, as well as at the vigil itself, there were also exorcisms, or prayers that the candidates may be freed from the powers of evil.

7 After their immersion into the baptismal pool, the newly baptized were anointed with oil, a symbol of the Holy Spirit who filled them with divine fire. Augustine is obviously enjoying this interplay among the sacramental symbols!

8 All references to the sacrament of the Eucharist.

9 An important dimension of Augustine's sacramental theology is the fact that all of the church's symbols and rituals point to the future. Christ is present and revealed through the sacraments. But Christ is also concealed by the sacramental symbols. At the end of time the Christ who is mysteriously present in the church's sacraments will be revealed in glory.

❧ Augustine's life as a priest and then bishop was filled with his sacramental ministry. He regularly presided and preached at the Eucharist. He baptized infants and adults during the Easter vigil service. He received penitents back into full communion with the church. He ordained priests and bishops.

Although the Catholic Church's explicit teaching about seven sacraments develops later in the Middle Ages, that theology draws upon Augustine's understanding of what a sacrament is. Every religion has its rituals and ceremonies. For Augustine, the liturgy of the church is a visible expression of the Word of God, calling believers into ever-deeper union with the Divine. Christians use simple material elements such as water, bread, wine, oil, and gestures in their liturgical services. Augustine taught that the deeper reality behind these signs and symbols is divine presence and grace. Christ continues his mission and ministry through the sacramental life of the church. So the church's sacraments are not just empty signs. Sacraments are the Word of God made visible for our benefit (see *Homilies on the Gospel of John* 80.3).

In this loaf of bread you are given clearly to understand how much you should love unity. I mean, was that loaf made from one grain? Weren't there many grains of wheat? But before they came into the loaf, they were all separate; they were joined together by means of water after a certain amount of pounding and crushing. Unless wheat is ground, after all, and moistened with water, it can't possibly get into this shape, which is called bread. In the same way, you too were being ground and pounded, as it were, by the humiliation of fasting and the sacrament of exorcism.[6] Then came baptism, and you were, in a manner of speaking, moistened with water in order to be shaped into bread. But it's not yet bread without fire to bake it. So what does fire represent? That's the chrism, the anointing. Oil, the fire feeder, you see, is the sacrament of the Holy Spirit.[7]

Sermon 227.1

So then, do you also wish to draw life from the Spirit of Christ? Be in the body of Christ.... That is why, when the apostle Paul is explaining this bread to us, he says, *We being many are one bread, one body* (1 Corinthians 10:17). O sacrament of piety, O sign of unity, O bond of charity![8] The one who wants to live has somewhere to live, has something to live on. Let him approach, let him believe, let him belong to the body so as to be given life.

Homilies on the Gospel of John 26.13

He shrouded his sacraments in mystery, willing them to be a hidden hope in the hearts of believers, to make a place where he might hide himself without in any way abandoning them, for in this darkness, where we still walk by faith, not by sight, we wait patiently in hope for what we do not see.[9]

Expositions of the Psalms 17.12

1 Both cities and towns had presiding bishops—even small towns. In some cases, bishops would ask a priest (also called a "presbyter") to administer a small parish church within the diocese. There were about three hundred Catholic bishops in North Africa in Augustine's time, and almost as many Donatist bishops.

2 Augustine often calls his Episcopal ministry a burden. As a scholar, he yearned for more time to study and write. As a monk, his heart's desire was to spend time in prayer and meditation. The duties of preaching, teaching, and pastoral care filled his days. Very often in the afternoon he would hear civil cases, not only for his parishioners but for other citizens as well—the Roman state permitted bishops to do so because the court system was so slow and often corrupt. It was at night, by the light of lamps burning "good, African olive oil," as he once remarked while in Italy, that he did most of his writing.

3 We have many letters and sermons in which Augustine expresses his harsh criticism of clerics who abused their rank or position. As the regional bishop with wider authority, he often acted to remove such men from the ministry.

4 A reference to his little community in Thagaste.

5 Had Augustine stayed in his imperial appointment as *rhetor*, he could have risen higher in the empire. His successor as *rhetor* actually became emperor for a short while.

6 That is, a bishop.

☐ Ministry

In those of us who have been selected as bishops,[1] two things need to be differentiated: the fact that we are Christians and the fact that we have been put in charge of others. We are Christians for our own sake; we are in charge of others for their sake. Many people will be saved without ever being responsible for others, and their journey is easier because they carry less of a burden.[2] We bishops as individuals will be judged on our Christianity, but because we have been put in charge of others, we will be judged also on the quality of our stewardship over those we led. People whom God puts in charge of others must not use their authority for their own advantage but for the good of those they rule. A bishop who just enjoys being the boss and seeks his own honor and looks to his own conveniences is feeding himself, not the sheep.[3]

SERMON 46.2

I, whom by God's grace you see before you as your bishop, came to this city as a young man; many of you know that. I was looking for a place to establish a monastery and live there with my brothers.[4] I had in fact left behind all worldly hopes, and I did not wish to be what I could have been;[5] nor, however, was I seeking to be what I am now. [6] *I have chosen to be a nobody in the house of my God, rather than to dwell in the tents of sinners* (Psalm 84:10). I separated myself from those who love the world; but I did not put myself on an equal footing with those who preside over churches. Nor did I choose a higher place at the banquet of my Lord, but a lower, insignificant one; and he was pleased to say to me, *Go up higher* (Luke 14:10). So much though did I dread the episcopate, that since I had already begun to acquire a reputation of some weight among the

7 | Then, as now, in many Christian churches the three orders of ministry were deacon, priest, and bishop. There were also minor orders of reader, acolyte, subdeacon, and so forth.

8 | Augustine preached this sermon on the feast of the Epiphany, January 6, 425, just five years before his death. With an honesty and forthrightness that might surprise us today, he was putting before his congregation some problems about money that had arisen in his Episcopal monastery, and that deeply troubled the old bishop who through much of his life suffered from asthma.

In our review of Augustine's life, we noted how he was seized by the congregation in Hippo and presented to Bishop Valerius for ordination. This was the last thing Augustine himself wanted. His biographer, Possidius, wrote that Augustine broke down and was overcome with tears at this unwelcome turn of events. He requested a few months to return to Thagaste and prepare himself for service to God's people.

By March, he was back in Hippo and had begun to preach—something unusual in that era, since normally only bishops preached. Augustine requested of Valerius that he be allowed to continue to live in community with brother monks even as he began his priestly service. So Valerius gave Augustine a house with a garden to establish his monastery where he lived as a priest, the first instance of an urban monastery in the Western Church. When he became bishop in 395, Augustine moved to the bishop's house. There he required his assistant priests and deacons to give up their worldly goods and live with him in community—a unique arrangement in that century. Over the next thirty-five years, Augustine's community in Hippo not only served the people of that diocese well, it also sent well-prepared men to serve as bishops for many other dioceses in North Africa.

servants of God, I wouldn't go near a place where I knew there was no bishop. I avoided this job, and I did everything I could to assure my salvation in a lowly position, and not to incur the grave risks of a high one. But, as I said, a servant ought not to oppose his Lord. I came to this city to see a friend, whom I thought I could gain for God, to join us in the monastery. It seemed safe enough, because the place had a bishop. I was caught, I was made a priest, and by this grade I eventually came to the episcopate....[7]

I have talked at length; please excuse the talkativeness of old age, that is also the timidity of ill health. I, as you can see, have now grown old in years; ill health made me an old man long ago.[8] Still, if God is pleased with what I have said now, he will give me strength, I won't let you down. Pray for me, that as long as there is a soul in this body, and any kind of strength supplied to it, I may serve you in preaching the Word of God.

SERMON 355.2, 7

9 This quote is from a poignant letter written in 429 to Bishop Honoratus in Numidia, to the west of Hippo. The Vandal tribes had begun their invasion of Africa from Spain and were terrorizing the population. The question put to Augustine was whether or not clergy had the right to take refuge in fortified cities. Augustine's answer was that clergy should remain with their people who needed the Word of God preached to them and the sacraments of the church administered to them, especially in such difficult times. For Augustine, the essence of ministry is to preach the Word and to administer the sacraments. This was the duty of bishops and priests, even if it endangered their lives. A year after he wrote this letter, Augustine died in Hippo as it was under siege by the Vandals.

Let the servants of Christ, the ministers of his Word and sacrament, do what he commanded or permitted.... Let them offer nourishment to their fellow servants who they know cannot live otherwise.[9]

LETTER 228.2

Where I'm terrified by what I am for you, I am given comfort by what I am with you. For you I am a bishop; with you, after all, I am a Christian. The first is the name of an office undertaken, the second a name of grace; that one means danger, this one salvation. Finally, as if in the open sea, I am being tossed about by the stormy activity involved in that one; as I recall by whose blood I have been redeemed, I enter a safe harbor in the tranquil recollection of this one; and thus while toiling away at my own proper office, I take my rest in the marvelous benefit conferred on all of us in common.

SERMON 340.1

✎ We began Part Three with the topics of knowing and loving God. It is appropriate then to end this section with a reflection on prayer, for it is in and through prayer that our knowledge and love of God grows and deepens. Certainly this is true for Augustine. His *Confessions* are really one long prayer to God. Throughout his book *The Trinity*, which reflects on the nature of God, Augustine includes prayers for God's guidance in his thinking and writing. And his many sermons are examples of his teaching within the context of the public prayer of the church, which as bishop he led.

For Augustine, prayer is an internal experience that requires that we give it time and space in our busy lives. Yet we should balance our lives of prayer with the needs of those for whom we care—prayer must never be an excuse for a lack of active charity. He understands prayer to be an important part of the life of faith, and so is confident that God's Holy Spirit will draw us by grace to seek it and to cherish it.

1 This sermon, preached around 410 to 412, is a very long homily on the Trinity in which Augustine explains his analogy of memory, understanding, and will in reflecting on the Trinity. These words come at the end of the sermon as he encourages people to prayerful reflection on God's Word. Philosophical or theological reflections on the nature of God are not substitutes for the experience and practice of prayer, which is a personal lifting of mind and heart to God.

2 This idea that we share with others what we discover in prayer is also found in Thomas Aquinas. Thomas was a medieval theologian who taught at the University of Paris and who wrote the famous *Summa Theologica* in which he presents his comprehensive review of Christian teaching. He wrote that true religious teaching is to share with others the fruits of our contemplation. The teaching or writing of any religious leader needs to arise from his or her own deep, prayerful experience of God to be authentic and compelling to others.

☐ Prayer

Let's leave something as well for people's reflections, let's generously allow something also to silence. Return to yourself, withdraw from all the din. Look inside yourself and see if you have there any pleasant private nook in your consciousness where you don't make a row, where you don't go to law, where you don't prepare your case, where you don't brood on pigheaded quarrels. Be gentle in hearing the Word, in order to understand.[1]

SERMON 52.22

No one should spend so much time in contemplation that they ignore the needs of a neighbor, nor be so absorbed in action that they feel no need for contemplation of God. What should draw us to contemplation is not escape or laziness, but the opportunity to search for and discover truth, knowing that as we make progress in this search, we share our discoveries with others.[2]

CITY OF GOD XIX.19

3 These three postures, kneeling, prostration, and elevation of the hands, were common postures for prayer among Christians in Augustine's time.

4 The desire for Sabbath means a desire to love God and to love each other. For Augustine, true prayer is rooted in and flows from such love.

5 This passage from *Confessions* recounts a mystical experience shared by Augustine and his mother shortly before her death. Augustine strives in words to express an experience that is ultimately beyond words and that is a temporary sharing in the eternal, infinite life of God. Augustine was a mystic, that is, someone who had profound experiences of the presence of God that took him above and out of normal human experience into ecstasy. This ecstasy, found in many religious traditions, is a state of being "out of" oneself and immersed in the immensity of the Infinite One.

This passage is unique in Christian mystical literature since it recounts an experience of shared ecstasy between Augustine and his mother. The ecstatic experiences of most other mystics are usually described as solitary events.

Such mystical experiences were certainly part of what Augustine meant when he describes the effect of God's grace calling us to God's love and delighting us by it. Augustine tells us that such experiences were a continuing part of his life of prayer: "From time to time you lead me into an inward experience quite unlike any other, a sweetness beyond understanding. If ever it is brought to fullness in me my life will not be what it is now, though what it will be I cannot tell" (*Confessions* X.40.65). Such mystical experiences are not just the prerogative of clergy, monks, and nuns. They are meant for all Christians—indeed all persons—since grace is given to all.

If your desire is continuous, your prayer is continuous, too. The apostle meant what he said, *Pray without ceasing* (1 Thessalonians 5:17). But can we be on our knees all the time, or prostrate ourselves continuously, or be holding up our hands uninterruptedly, that he bids us, *Pray without ceasing*?[3] If we say that these things constitute prayer, I do not think we can pray without ceasing. But there is another kind of prayer that never ceases, an interior prayer that is desire. Whatever else you may be engaged upon, if you are all the while desiring that Sabbath, you never cease to pray. If you do not want to interrupt your prayer, let your desire be uninterrupted. Your continuous desire is your continuous voice.[4] You will only fall silent if you stop loving.... The chilling of charity is the silence of the heart; the blazing of charity is the heart's clamor.

Expositions of the Psalms 37.14

We stood leaning against a window that looked out on a garden within the house where we were staying at Ostia on the Tiber, for there, far from the crowds, we were recruiting our strength after the long journey, in preparation for our voyage overseas.[5] We were alone, conferring very intimately. Forgetting what lay in the past, and stretching out to what was ahead, we inquired between ourselves in the light of present truth, the Truth, which is yourself, what the eternal life of the saints would be like....

6 This phrase, "That Which Is" (*idipsum* in Latin) calls to mind the mystical Hindu phrase for God, *Tat Tvam Asi*—"That Thou Art" or "That Art Thou" from the Chandogya Upanishad (6.8.7).

7 Augustine ends the first book of his *Confessions* with this beautiful prayer that asks God's blessing on his spiritual and personal growth and thanks God for the simple fact of his existence.

Our colloquy led us to the point where the pleasures of the body's sense, however intense and in however brilliant a material light enjoyed, seemed unworthy not merely of comparison but even of remembrance beside the joy of that life, and we lifted ourselves in longing yet more ardent toward *That Which Is,* and step by step traversed all bodily creatures and heaven itself, whence sun and moon and stars shed their light upon the earth.[6] Higher still we mounted by inward thought and wondering discourse on your works, and we arrived at the summit of our own minds; and this too we transcended, to touch that land of never-failing plenty where you pasture Israel forever with the food of truth. Life there is the Wisdom through whom all these things are made, and all others that have been or ever will be forever. Rather should we say that in her there is no "has been" or "will be," but only being, for she is eternal, but past and future do not belong to eternity. And as we talked and panted for it, we just touched the edge of it by the utmost leap of our hearts; then, sighing and unsatisfied, we left the first fruits of our spirit captive there, and returned to the noise of articulate speech, where a word has beginning and end. How different from your Word, our Lord, who abides in himself, and grows not old, but renews all things.

CONFESSIONS IX.10.24

But I give thanks to you, my sweetness, my honor, my confidence; to you, my God, I give thanks for your gifts. Do you preserve them for me. So will you preserve me too, and what you have given me will grow and reach perfection, and I will be with you; because this, too, is your gift to me—that I exist.[7]

CONFESSIONS I.20.31

Part Four: While in the World

1 Augustine affirms two things in this paragraph: God created out of eternal love and infinite goodness. However, creation is not the same as the eternal being that is God. This is the classic distinction in the Abrahamic faiths between God and creation. While creation reflects and reveals aspects of God, it is not in itself divine, but the result of a totally gratuitous act of the divine will.

2 This is a reference to the text of Genesis 1:2, which states that in the beginning the earth was formless and empty, that darkness covered the abyss, and that the Spirit of God hovered over the waters of the abyss. Augustine taught that God created *ex nihilo*, that is, out of nothing. But this was a two-step process, according to Genesis. First, God created formless matter and spirit, which Genesis describes as the abyss. Second, the Spirit of God brought form to matter and spirit. With the creation of form, beings emerged from the abyss in their distinctiveness. Augustine explains that this was not a temporal sequence, not two creative acts, but two dimensions of bringing creation into being.

3 In their receiving form and distinctive nature, all elements of creation are thereby called into relationship with the Creator through the Word of God, the second person of the Trinity. While Augustine reflects on how the Word and the Spirit played different roles in divine creation as described in Genesis, the persons of the Trinity are present in each other and so all worked together in each dimension of the creative process.

4 Only God is unchanging and unchangeable, according to Augustine and other Christian writers.

☐ Creation

Solely by your abundant goodness has your creation come to be and stood firm, for you did not want so good a thing to be missing. It could be of no profit to you, nor equal to yourself as though proceeding from your own substance, yet there was the possibility of its existing as your creation.[1] What advance claim did heaven and earth have upon you, when you made them in the Beginning? Let your spiritual and corporeal creation speak up and tell us what rights they had. In your Wisdom you made them, so that on your Wisdom might depend even those inchoate, formless beings, whether of the spiritual or the corporeal order, beings plunging into excess or straying into far-off regions of unlikeness to yourself.[2] Even in its unformed state, the spiritual was of higher dignity than any formed corporeal thing, and a corporeal being, even unformed, had more dignity than if it had had no existence at all. Thus these formless things would have depended on your Word even had they not by that same Word been summoned back to your unity and received form and become, every one of them, exceedingly good because they are from you, the one supreme Good.[3]

CONFESSIONS XIII.2.2

Heaven and earth plainly exist, and by the very fact that they undergo change and variation, they cry out that they were made.[4] If anything was not made, yet exists, there is no element in it that was not present earlier; for change and variation imply that something is made that was not previously there. Heaven and earth further proclaim that they did not make themselves: "We are, because we have been made; we did not exist before we came to be, as though to bring ourselves into being."

145

5 In this long sentence, Augustine is saying that the process of our creation as human beings continues through the work of grace, which enlightens our minds about the Creator and empowers our hearts to journey in faith and love back to the One who made us. Our life, in and of itself, is not "beatitude," that is, not necessarily and always happy or blessed. Indeed, most of us live through dark and turbulent struggles at different times. It is creative grace that leads us eventually to be "perfected, illumined, and beatified"—Augustine's language for our ultimate destiny in God.

6 In developing his theology of creation from the text of Genesis, Augustine had to reconcile the fact that scripture does not mention most of the great variety of living things in nature. So he writes about *rationes seminales*, causal formulae, or potentialities that God planted in the first creatures so that new species could develop later in the time allotted by God. This is not the same as the theory of evolution, nor is it exactly the same as what has been called intentional design. Rather, Augustine is accommodating his knowledge of the physical world with the text of Genesis in a way that affirms the ongoing process of creation by God. This idea of the potential development of new species from *rationes seminales* is also found in the writings of the Stoics and Neoplatonists.

And their visible existence is the voice with which they say this. It was you who made them, Lord: you are beautiful, so it must have been you, because they are beautiful; you who are good must have made them, because they are good; you who are, because they are.

CONFESSIONS XI.4.6

What, then, would have been lacking to that Good, which is your very self, even if these things had never come to be at all, or had remained in their unformed state? It was no need on your part that drove you to make them. Out of your sheer goodness you controlled them and converted them to their form; it was not as though your own happiness stood in need of completion by them.... Rather, did your unassailable, immutable will, sufficient in itself unto itself, brood over the life you had made, over the creature for which life is not the same as beatitude, for it is alive even in its own dark turbulence; but it has the prospect of being converted to him who made it, that so it may live more and more fully on the fount of life, and in his light see light, and so be perfected, illumined, and beatified.[5]

CONFESSIONS XIII.4.5

It is our business to inquire about how those causal formulae were set, with which he primed the universe when he first created all things simultaneously.[6] Was it so that all things that come to birth in the way we see, whether shrubs or animals, would go through the different intervals of time appropriate to each species in its taking shape and its growth; or so that they would be fully formed forthwith, in the way it is believed that Adam was made without any growing pains in adult manhood? But why should we not believe that those formulae contained each potentiality, so that anything would be actualized from them that pleased the one who would make them?

THE LITERAL MEANING OF GENESIS VI.14.25

7 Augustine mentions in a number of texts his admiration for and astonishment at the beauty, complexity, and efficiency of insect life. He also warns against destroying seemingly useless pests such as flies, mosquitoes, and larvae. In an admonition that seems to anticipate the contemporary environmental movement, he warns that we should respect every species of life. Otherwise, "whether in ignorance of the place they hold in nature, or, though we know it, sacrificing them to our own convenience" we destroy the balance of nature intended by God (*City of God* XI.16).

8 In this passage, Augustine addresses the question of the miracles attributed to Jesus and other biblical figures. He certainly believes in those miracles, but turns his readers' attention to the miracles of creation that surround us every day, but that may fail to astonish us because we take them for granted.

❧ Augustine's theology of creation is both simple and complex. It is simple because it can be summed up in a few direct statements. God created everything that exists. Everything that exists is good in its own way and according to its own purpose—from the simplest bit of matter or speck of life, to the grandest sweep of the heavens. Everything that exists came into being simply because of God's loving goodness, and everything continues in being by God's loving will.

Augustine's theology of creation is complex because he elaborates it by close commentary on the first few chapters of the book of Genesis. While he references earlier philosophers and other Christian theologians, Augustine forges his own distinctive teaching about creation on the anvil of the scriptural text. A reader familiar with contemporary methods of textual analysis will find Augustine's commentaries on Genesis sometimes poetic and inspiring, at other times excessive and exotic, and always guided by his fourth- and fifth-century understanding of the Hebrew Bible narrative.

[E]very creature has a special beauty proper to its nature, and when one ponders the matter well, these creatures are a cause of intense admiration and enthusiastic praise of their all-powerful Maker.... God creates them tiny in body, keen in sense, and full of life, so that we may feel a deeper wonder at the agility of a mosquito on the wing than at the size of a beast of burden on the hoof, and may admire more intensely the works of the smallest ants than the burdens of the camels.[7]

THE LITERAL MEANING OF GENESIS III.14.22

Shall I speak of the manifold and various loveliness of sky and earth and sea; of the plentiful supply and wonderful qualities of the light; of sun, moon, and stars; of the shade of trees, of the colors and perfume of flowers; of the multitude of birds, all differing in plumage and in song; of the variety of animals, of which the smallest in size are often the most wonderful—the works of ants and bees astonishing us more than the huge bodies of whales? Shall I speak of the sea, which itself is so grand a spectacle when it arrays itself as it were in vestures of various colors, now running through every shade of green and again becoming purple or blue? Is it not delightful to look at it in a storm?...

CITY OF GOD XXII.24

Think of the alternation of day and night and the undeviating pattern of the heavenly bodies, the four seasons of the year, the fall and return of the leaves of the trees, the infinite power of seeds, the beauty of light and colors and sounds and smells, and the variety of tastes. Imagine being able to talk to someone who saw and experienced these things for the first time. That person would be astonished and overwhelmed by the miracles. We, on the other hand, think little of all these things.... I call a miracle any event that is so difficult or extraordinary as to be beyond the expectation or power of those it astonishes.[8]

THE ADVANTAGE OF BELIEVING 16.34

1 "Concupiscence" is a word Augustine uses often. In modern English, concupiscence means sexual desire or ardent, sensuous longing. For Augustine, the Latin verb *concupiscere* means to desire strongly, and he uses it to describe sexual desire, including his own. But there are two other kinds of concupiscence that Augustine identifies. These are concupiscence of the eyes or idle curiosity and worldly pride or ambition. Concupiscence in its broadest Augustinian meaning refers to a rupture in or corruption of our relationship with some aspect of creation. Concupiscence of the flesh is the inordinate misuse of our sexual nature as embodied beings. Concupiscence of the eyes is the useless accumulation of meaningless information that is not part of our search for truth or proper stewardship of creation, but rather a distraction from the value of truth, the dignity of persons, and the integrity of nature. Prideful ambition is an inflated sense of who we are and what we are owed in the greater scheme of life based on flattery or social position.

Concupiscence is what drives us to violate the order inherent in proper loving, which we explored on pages 40–41. Concupiscence leads to destructive disorder in our relationships with each other, in the fabric of society, and in our living with nature.

2 Concupiscence of the flesh is sexual desire, natural in itself, but destructive when it overrides other dimensions of a loving, committed relationship, or when it is the only reason for a relationship. In Book VI of *Confessions,* Augustine describes how his strong sexual desires complicated life in his early thirties. At Monica's insistence, he dismisses the mother of his son after almost fourteen years of a loving relationship so that he can be engaged to an underage girl from a proper family. Since he must wait for two years until the marriage, he takes up with yet another woman. He describes himself as "no lover of marriage but the slave of lust" (VI.15.25).

☐ Concupiscence

Quite certainly you command me to refrain from concupiscence of the flesh and concupiscence of the eyes and worldly pride.[1]

CONFESSIONS X.30.41

It was my habitual attempt to sate an insatiable concupiscence that for the most part savagely tormented me and held me captive....[2]

CONFESSIONS VI.12.22

3 This passage is remarkable in its frankness. Here is a forty-something, famous bishop of the Catholic Church admitting that he still struggles with sexual urges while both awake and asleep.

However, Augustine is taking the opportunity of his continuing struggles with celibacy to make a particular point. For him, as for other ancient thinkers, sexual desire was an inferior part of our rational nature because it overwhelmed our ability to reason and interfered with our will to choose. In Augustine's view, the power of sexual desire is the most common and most obvious example of the disorder in our nature and in our relationship with God ever since the sin of Adam and Eve. Sexual concupiscence is a result of original sin, according to Augustine. He even posits that though Adam and Eve had sex as the natural way of propagating the human race before the Fall, their sexual union was "without the tumultuous ardor of lust" (*The Literal Meaning of Genesis* IX.3.6). Sex in Eden was loving but perfunctory—a curious conclusion at best.

On the other hand, unlike many early Christian writers who disparaged sex and marriage, Augustine taught that sexual activity for the purpose of procreation is not evil because it is part of God's will for creation. Nonetheless, the original sin of Adam and Eve is responsible for the way we now experience sexual desire, with its powerful urges that overwhelm our rationality and often lead us into hurtful behavior. Lust is ever a reminder of the original sin that clouds our reason and cowers our will (*The Literal Meaning of Genesis* XI.1.3).

Victims of sexual aggression, infidelity, or injustice might find some truth in Augustine's writings about concupiscence of the flesh. However, to develop a more positive Christian theology of human sexuality one must return to other sources such as Hebrew scripture and the writings of Christian mystics. Augustine's pessimistic view of sexuality left subsequent centuries of Christians with an abiding, and often unhealthy, view of human sexuality.

Yet in my memory, of which I have spoken at length, sexual images survive, because they were imprinted there by former habit.[3] While I am awake, they suggest themselves feebly enough, but in dreams with power to arouse me not only to pleasurable sensations but even to consent, to something closely akin to the act they represent.... Is your hand not powerful enough to heal all my soul's ills, all-powerful God, and by a still more generous grace to extinguish unruly stirring even in my sleep? Yes, Lord, you will heap gift after gift upon me, that my soul may shake itself free from the sticky morass of concupiscence and follow me to you. As for those foul obscenities in my dreams, where bestial imagination drives the flesh to the point of polluting itself, grant that this soul of mine, through your grace rebellious against itself no more, may not even consent to, still less, commit them.

CONFESSIONS X.30.41–42

4 Notice that Augustine considers concupiscence of the mind "more fraught with danger" than lust. But how can curiosity and inquisitiveness be so dangerous? Was not Augustine himself endlessly curious about the meaning of life and the glories of creation? His point here is about motivation. If we want information about others to use it against them in idle gossip or intentional hurt, we are guilty of this second type of concupiscence. If we accumulate information without purpose or direction, or jealously hoard facts to better others in argument, we are not helping in the common search for truth for which we have all been created. Just as sexual misconduct is a misuse of God's gift of our body, Augustine believes that we betray our noble capacity to think and reason carefully by exercising it aimlessly or selfishly.

5 Some contemporary phenomena illustrate this concupiscence of the eyes: for example, the bizarre tabloids and gossip magazines at the grocery checkout, or endless webpages that seem to have no context for or validation of the information they present, or the angry propaganda in media outlets whose purpose is not rational engagement with others but irrational fear of difference. None of these "morbid cravings" or "frivolous fascinations" (*Confessions* X.35.55–56) enrich or ennoble our humanity.

6 Augustine would have enjoyed much flattery and empty praise in his position as *rhetor* in the imperial court. Though he abandoned that professional success upon his conversion and retired to a hidden life back in the little community he set up in Thagaste, within a few years he finds himself once again in a position of authority and leadership as bishop of Hippo. So once more he is vulnerable to believing the praise heaped upon him by others. He admits to this temptation as something he struggles with. The "enemy" mentioned in this paragraph who seeks to trap Augustine is the devil.

There is still another temptation, one more fraught with danger. In addition to the concupiscence of the flesh, which lures us to indulge in the pleasures of all the senses and brings disaster on its slaves who flee far from you, there is also concupiscence of the mind, a frivolous, avid curiosity.[4] Though it works through these same senses, it is a craving not for gratification of the flesh but for experience through the flesh. It masquerades as a zeal for knowledge and learning. Since it is rooted in a thirst for firsthand information about everything, and since the eyes are paramount among the senses in acquiring information, this inquisitive tendency is called in holy scripture *concupiscence of the eyes* (1 John 2:16)....[5] My life is full of such weaknesses, and my sole hope is your exceedingly great mercy. When our heart becomes a bin for things like this, stuffed with a load of idle rubbish, our prayers are often interrupted and disturbed by it....

CONFESSIONS X.35.54, 57

[Pride] is the temptation to want veneration and affection from others, and to want them not for the sake of some quality that merits them, but in order to make such admiration itself the cause of my joy. It is no true joy at all, but leads only to a miserable life and shameful ostentation....

The enemy of our true happiness therefore lies in wait for those of us who by reason of our official positions in human society must of necessity be loved and honored by our fellows.[6] On every side, he scatters popular plaudits to trap us, so that as we eagerly collect them we may be caught unawares and abandon our delight in your truth to look for it instead in human flattery. So the affection and honor we receive come to be something we enjoy not for your sake but in your stead....

7 Augustine sums up the three kinds of concupiscence, warning that pride is more dangerous than lust or curiosity. In all three cases, however, it is God's grace that woos our minds and hearts away from destructive desires and back to true love and loving truth. Grace is the cure for the three kinds of ills that afflict us. Grace heals and restores us to love, truth, and humility

In this respect, too, you lay upon us the injunction to continence: so give what you command, and then command whatever you will.... Where sensual desires or idle curiosity are concerned, I can measure my progress in self-restraint by going without these pleasures, either voluntarily or because opportunity for indulgence is lacking.... But what of praise?... What indeed, except that I do enjoy being praised? But I take more delight in truth itself than in any eulogy....[7]

CONFESSIONS X.36.59–37.60

1 To understand the importance of this sentence, you must recall how important friendship is for Augustine. See pages 101–107 of this book. The love of friendship, as experienced between spouses, is a particular revelation of God who is love.

2 We are all related because we all come from Adam and Eve.

3 Augustine makes a distinction here between the "union" of husband and wife, by which he means their mutual love and friendship, and sexual intercourse, which produces children. Thus, Augustine affirms the *central reality* of marriage to be the mutual love and friendship enjoyed by the spouses. Elsewhere in the same book he writes that a marriage with no children is still a full marriage (*The Excellence of Marriage* 5.5).

However, he repeatedly says the *primary purpose* of marriage is the procreation of children. The limitations of his fourth- and fifth-century Christian intellectual milieu, and perhaps his own sexual history, never allow him to make a theological affirmation of sexual intercourse as a natural, healthy, and wholesome expression of mutual love and friendship.

4 While Augustine affirms the spiritual equality of men and women in their capacities for love and friendship, he reflects the New Testament teaching and the social understanding of his time that women are to be submissive to their husbands.

☐ Marriage

Every human being is part of the human race, and human nature is a social entity and has naturally the great benefit and power of friendship.[1] For this reason, God wished to produce all persons out of one, so that they would be held together in their social relationships not only by similarity of race, but also by the bond of kinship.[2] The first natural bond of human society, therefore, is that of husband and wife.... For those who walk together, and look ahead together to where they are walking, do so at each other's side. The result is the bonding of society in its children, and this is the one honorable fruit, not of the union of husband and wife, but of their sexual conjunction.[3] For even without that kind of intimacy, there could have been between the two sexes a certain relationship of friendship and kinship where one is in charge and the other compliant.[4]

THE EXCELLENCE OF MARRIAGE 1.1

5 Here again he affirms that the central reality of a marriage is the relationship of the spouses. By calling this relationship sacramental, Augustine is affirming the love between the spouses as a sign of God's love. Even if that relationship produces no children, the sacramental marriage bond cannot be broken, even to enter another marriage for the purpose of having children. It would be almost another thousand years before the Catholic Church officially taught that marriage was one of the seven sacraments, at the Council of Florence in the 1430s.

6 In this last phrase, and in subsequent selections, Augustine expresses his belief that marriage provides a safe environment for the satisfaction of sexual concupiscence.

7 Augustine's teaching that sexual intercourse is a venial sin when not engaged for procreation became standard Catholic teaching for centuries. A venial sin is a minor sin, or one committed without deliberate intent. Since sexual concupiscence overrides our rationality, according to this view, it impedes our full consent and ameliorates our guilt.

While all this seems strange to modern sensibilities, we have to consider the historical context in which Augustine developed his theology. He was actually defending sexual intercourse against people like Jerome, who taught that it was seriously sinful in itself.

8 In this last sentence, Augustine affirms the superiority of virginity and celibacy against Jovinian. This point of view led to centuries of belief in Catholicism and other Christian sects that nuns, monks, and celibate priests were spiritually superior to married laypeople. On this point, Augustine wrote that a charitable and just married person was spiritually superior to an uncharitable and unjust virgin or widow. In his book *Holy Virginity,* he consistently admonishes those who live as celibates for the sake of the Gospel to realize their dependence on grace and practice the virtue of humility. Nonetheless, the superiority of celibate religious persons persists as an often unquestioned popular belief in Catholic Christianity.

The good of marriage, in fact, is threefold: fidelity, offspring, sacrament. What fidelity means is that neither partner should sleep with another person outside the marriage bond; offspring means that children should be welcomed with love, brought up with kindness, given a religious education; sacrament means that the union should not be broken up, and that if either husband or wife is sent away, neither should marry another even for the sake of having children.[5] This is, so to speak, the set-square of marriage, good either for embellishing the fertility of nature or putting straight the crookedness of lust.[6]

THE LITERAL MEANING OF GENESIS IX.7.12

When the performance of the marriage duty is insisted on unreasonably, so that they have intercourse even when it is not for the purpose of having children, the apostle allows this as something that can be excused, though it is not something he lays down as a command (1 Corinthians 7:6). So, even if a perverted morality motivates them to have intercourse like that, marriage still saves them from adultery or fornication. It is not that conduct of that kind is accepted because of marriage, but it is forgiven because of marriage. Married people, therefore, not only owe each other fidelity in relation to sexual union for the sake of having children, which in this mortal state is the human race's first social union, but also in a certain way they owe each other a mutual service to relieve each other's weakness, and thereby avoid illicit unions. As a result, even if one of them favors permanent abstinence, this is not possible unless the other agrees to it.... Marital intercourse for the sake of procreating children is not sinful. When it is for the purpose of satisfying sensuality, but still with one's spouse, because there is marital fidelity, it is a venial sin.[7] Adultery or fornication, however, is a mortal sin. For this reason, abstinence from all sexual union is better even than marital intercourse performed for the sake of procreating.[8]

THE EXCELLENCE OF MARRIAGE 6.6

9 The practice of granting annulments in the Catholic Church and in many other Christian denominations takes account of other human failings besides sexual concupiscence. Thus, reasons for annulments include addictions, serious personality disorders, and mental illnesses that impair a person's capacity for the love and friendship necessary to enter the marriage bond in the first place. Such pastoral considerations were not part of church practice in Augustine's time.

✒ Augustine's theology of marriage emerges out of a theological debate about whether marriage itself was good.

Jovinian, himself a celibate monk, nevertheless taught that virginity and celibacy were not superior to marriage. All Christians were sanctified by baptism. The ascetical life practiced by virgins or widows gave them no special status or merit. Jovinian was concerned about the growth of popular ascetical practice in the Roman Church, as the period of persecution and trial by the pre–Christian Roman Empire passed into history in the early fourth century. Strict asceticism and celibacy were a kind of new martyrdom.

The bishop of Rome summoned his clergy to consider Jovinian's point of view. They promptly condemned it as heretical. Virgins and widows had a special place in the church and a superior status in terms of virtue.

That official declaration against Jovinian wasn't enough for Saint Jerome. From his monastic retreat in Bethlehem, Jerome took aim at Jovinian and fired a missile westward in the form of his treatise *Against Jovinian*. This polemical work had unfortunate collateral damage. Jerome ended up not only exalting virginity and celibacy but he actually denigrated marriage and found little if any good in it.

Augustine, as he so often did in theological disagreements, tried to find the mean between these two extremes. In two books written in 410, *The Excellence of Marriage* and *Holy Virginity*, Augustine affirms against Jerome the goodness of marriage as a gift of God established before the Fall of Adam and Eve in Eden. He also argues against Jovinian in favor of the superiority of virginity and celibacy.

Sexual union that is necessary for the purpose of having children is blameless, and it alone is part of marriage. If it goes beyond that necessity, it is no longer ruled by reason but by sensuality. Nevertheless, it is proper for married persons to accord this to their spouses, so that the spouses will not commit a mortal sin of adultery, though it is not proper to require it for themselves. If they are both overcome by this kind of sensuality, clearly they are not doing something that is part of marriage. Nevertheless, if in their intimacy they value what is honorable more than what is dishonorable, that is to say, what is part of marriage rather than what is not part of marriage, then on the authority of the apostle this is allowed to them as something excusable. Marriage does not encourage this fault, but it pleads for it.

THE EXCELLENCE OF MARRIAGE 10.11

Entering into the marriage contract is a matter of such sacredness that it is not annulled by ... separation. While the man lives, the woman he has left commits adultery if she marries someone else, and he who left her is the cause of that wrongdoing.... That bond of association between spouses is so strong that although it is tied for the purpose of having children, it is not untied for the same purpose of having children.[9]

THE EXCELLENCE OF MARRIAGE 7.7

1 A reference to Genesis 3:16–19, which identifies difficult toil and physical labor as a result of original sin and so outside Eden.

2 Augustine contradicts himself here. In the opening paragraph of *The Excellence of Marriage* (1.1), as we have seen (page 159), he writes about the friendship of husband and wife who walk together side by side. In his own life, he chose the friendship of celibate males in the monastery over the friendship of a wife. He extrapolates the superiority of his own choice, no doubt with a little help from Saint Paul who wrote to the Corinthians about his own preference for celibacy over marriage: "I wish that all of you were as I myself am" (1 Corinthians 7:1–7).

Perhaps if Augustine had a more positive understanding of human sexuality and its creative role in loving relationships, beyond procreation and a release for concupiscence within marriage, his theological legacy on the role of women would have been less destructive.

☐ Women

If it was not for help in producing children that a wife was made for the man, then what other help was she made for? If it was to till the earth together with him, there was as yet no hard toil to need such assistance; and if there had been the need, a male would have made a better help.[1] The same can be said about companionship, should he grow tired of solitude. How much more agreeably, after all, for conviviality and conversation would two male friends live together on equal terms than man and wife?...[2] For these reasons, I cannot work out what help a wife could have been made to provide the man with, if you take away the purpose of childbearing.

THE LITERAL MEANING OF GENESIS IX.5.9

3   Augustine tried to reconcile what the apostle Paul writes in 1 Corinthians 11:7, "The man ought not to cover his head, since he is the image and glory of God. But the woman is the glory of the man," with the equal status of male and female as images of God in Genesis 1:27. A contemporary biblical scholar would take a very different approach, first trying to understand what Paul wrote in the social context of the first century of Jewish Christianity.

4   This passage contains the paradox of Augustine's subordination of women and his assertion that spiritually they are equal to men. Both in scripture and in Augustine's writings, the theological subordination of women reflects the social and cultural subordination of women of the times. However, the dominance of male-authored writings that survived and prevailed throughout the process of the canonization of texts silenced Jewish and Christian writers more critical of the cultural and theological status quo. Contemporary historical, textual criticism gives us an advantage that Augustine did not have in his commentaries on scripture.

He also writes that male-female sexual differences will be part of the resurrection of the dead, though the physical and social subordination of women will not (*City of God* XXII.17, 18; *Expositions of the Psalms* 188.2). To that extent, he predicts liberation from such social constraints.

5   Augustine uses human reason and will to establish the equality of women and men. However, his conflicted and restricted understanding of human sexuality prevents him from developing a healthy theology of the body. He never seems to connect his very positive theology of creation as good with a potential theology of the body as good. Concupiscence gets in the way, until the resurrection of the body.

But we must say how what the apostle says about the man and not the woman being the image of God avoids contradicting what is written in Genesis: *God made man to the image of God; he made him male and female; he made them and blessed them* (Genesis 1:27).[3] It says that what was made to the image of God is the human nature that is realized in each sex, and it does not exclude the female from the image of God that is meant. For after saying *God made man to the image of God*, it says *he made them male and female*—or at least with the other punctuation, *male and female he made them*. So how are we to take what we have heard from the apostle, that the man is the image of God, and so he is forbidden to cover his head, but the woman is not and so she is told to do so?... [T]he woman with her husband is the image of God in such a way that the whole of that substance is one image, but when she is assigned her function of being an assistant, which is her concern alone, she is not the image of God; whereas in what concerns the man alone, he is the image of God as fully and completely as when the woman is joined to him in one whole.[4]

THE TRINITY XII.3.10

After all, the authority of the apostle as well as plain reason assures us that man was not made to the image of God as regards the shape of his body, but as regards his rational mind. It is an idle and base kind of thinking that supposes that God is confined with the limits of a body with features and limbs.... Man was not made to the image of him who created him as regards his body or any old part of his consciousness, but as regards the rational mind, which is capable of recognizing God.[5]

6 Augustine distinguishes between two types of human knowing: *scientia* or knowledge; and *sapientia* or wisdom (*The Trinity* XIII.6.24). Knowledge is the attention given by reason to the practical affairs of life and survival in this world. It includes the liberal arts and sciences, as well as the practical arts of the professions. Wisdom is the attention given by reason to God and the journey of faith toward God. Woman and her head-covering, as mandated by Saint Paul, symbolizes knowledge. Man, with head uncovered, symbolizes wisdom.

Though Augustine writes that men and women both partake in knowledge and wisdom, the symbolic identification of women with what he considers the lesser of the two is problematic. Even on the level of reason, Augustine subordinates women. Though he certainly considers women fully capable of wisdom, he forges a powerful symbol of the archetypal feminine alloyed with things of this world and the archetypal masculine with things of heaven. This symbolic identification, coupled with his inability to connect love and sexuality, are an unintended source of misogyny in subsequent centuries. It is not too difficult to imagine that Augustine himself would have been distressed by the role of his writings in the mistreatment of women.

7 In 413 or 414, Augustine wrote a long, book-length letter to Paulina, a Catholic laywoman in Africa. He wrote in response to a theological question she posed about what it means to "see God." Augustine's respect for Paulina's intelligence and faith is obvious in the care he takes to develop his argument and in his references to other theological writings of the day. He also acknowledges that Paulina herself will take his ideas to other Christians for discussion and debate. This is only one example of many letters Augustine wrote to women who had posed spiritual or moral questions to him and illustrates the difference between Augustine's theoretical distinctions about knowledge and wisdom, and his actual relationships with women of his time.

Now it is with respect to this renewal that we are also made sons of God through Christian baptism, and when we put on the new man, it is of course Christ that we put on through faith. Is there anyone then who would exclude females from this association, seeing that together with us men they are fellow heirs of grace?... Well, it is only because she differs from the man in the sex of her body that her bodily covering could suitably be used to symbolize that part of the reason that is diverted to the management of temporal things, signifying that the mind of man does not remain the image of God except in the part that adheres to the eternal ideas to contemplate or consult them: and it is clear that females have this as well as males. So in their minds, a common nature is to be acknowledged; but in their bodies, the distribution of the one mind is symbolized.[6]

THE TRINITY XII.3.12

This introduction of mine does not yet examine the question you posed, but it prepares you and others who will read these ideas as to what sort of judge you ought to be of my writings or of those of any others.[7]

LETTER 147.5

❧ Augustine's political theology was shaped by the political and social forces of his time and place. The invasion of the city of Rome by the Visigoths, as we have seen, led Augustine to reflect for many years on the role of empire and the meaning of political power. He integrates his understandings of sin, grace, and salvation into his review of wider social and historical movements.

1 Augustine's understanding of history and politics is based on his theology of the will. The course of human events is not determined by submission to pagan gods and idol worship, as the Roman imperial cult suggested. Nor is it the result of blind fate as some philosophers taught. The directions of history are the results of human choice. We are responsible. "The times are evil, the times are troubled, that's what people say. Let us live good lives, and the times are good. We ourselves are the times. Whatever we are like, that's what the times are like" (*Sermon* 80.8). Augustine believed that if we choose the good and the right as individuals guided and strengthened by God's grace, then social structures, laws, and states will strengthen and grow for the benefit of all. If we choose selfishly and poorly, society weakens and all suffer.

2 The City of God, or the Heavenly City, is not coextensive with any one state or country, culture or people, form of government, societal organization, or religion. It is to be found everywhere in the world, sometimes hidden, sometimes obvious. It happens whenever and wherever individuals and groups exercise their freedom to choose the right and the good. Those choices for the right and the good are, in Augustine's way of thinking, enlightened and strengthened by God's grace, which is active in all persons, all nations, all religions.

3 The City of God in this world can be recognized by its chief characteristic: peace. Augustine does not argue in support of any one political structure. As a bishop, he only hopes that his church can live in freedom to follow its conscience in a society good enough to allow for that religious freedom. He understands the achievement of such tolerance and peace in society to require political compromise.

☐ Politics

Two loves built two cities: the earthly city created by love of self, carried to the point of contempt for God; and the Heavenly City, created by love of God, carried to the point of contempt for self.[1]

CITY OF GOD XIV.28

All the while the Heavenly City lives in exile on this earth, it recruits citizens from every nation, gathering a society of aliens who speak all languages. It takes no account of the differences in their customs, laws, and institutions, by which earthly peace is established or maintained. It suppresses none of them, destroys none. Rather, it maintains and observes everything that, though different in different nations, tends to one and the same end, earthly peace, at least provided nothing impedes the religion that teaches us to worship the one true and sovereign God.[2]

Thus the Heavenly City in its pilgrimage makes use of earthly peace, and in all that concerns our mortal nature, it defends and seeks the compromise of human wills, so far as may be permitted without detriment to true religion and piety.[3] In fact, that city relates this earthly peace to the heavenly peace, which is so truly peaceful that it should be considered the only peace deserving the name, at least as regards rational creatures. It is the perfectly ordered and completely harmonious fellowship in the enjoyment of God, and of one another in God. When we arrive at that state of peace, life will no longer end in death, but will be a life in sure and sober truth; and there will be no

4 | Earthly peace is a foretaste of the peace of heaven. Note that in Augustine's theology, perfect peace will be attained only in heaven, because only in heaven will concupiscence of lust, pride, and idle curiosity, which drive us to bad choices, be finally conquered (see chapter on concupiscence, especially page 152).

5 | This is Augustine's definition of a people or state. He identifies the relative value of a political entity by focusing not on its past achievements, nor on its military might, nor on its wealth. Rather, a state's purpose or ends are the measure of its value.

6 | Augustine is disagreeing here with the approach of Cicero and Sallust. They argued that when a state deteriorates into the dysfunction that characterized much of Roman history, it is no longer a state or commonwealth. Augustine says it remains a state or commonwealth, just not a very good or effective one. Augustine thereby argues for the reality of good and bad political structures, depending on the quality of their objectives or ends.

7 | In *City of God*, Augustine takes the politics and aggression of building an empire to task. He traces the progress of the Assyrian, Macedonian, and Roman Empires, affirming that God can use even the wayward aims of empires to advance the purposes of the divine will in human history. He believed that while the *Pax Romana* may have allowed for the spread of the Christian faith, it is no reason to glorify the Roman Empire. In fact, on this earth all those citizens of the City of God, who live in any society trying to make good choices, are pilgrims on their way to becoming citizens of heaven. "The City of God lives amid the city of this world, as far as its human element is concerned. But it lives there as an alien sojourner" (*City of God* XVIII.1).

animal body to weigh down the soul in its corruption, but a spiritual body free of cravings and subdued to the will in every way.[4]

The Heavenly City, while on pilgrimage in faith possesses this peace, and by virtue of that faith lives a life of righteousness, with the attainment of that peace in view in every good action performed in relation to God and to neighbor, since the life of a city is inevitably a social life.

City of God XIX.17

If a "people" is the association of a multitude of rational beings united by common agreement on the objects of their love, then it follows that to observe the character of a particular people we must examine the objects of their love.... The better the objects of this agreement, the better the people; the worse the objects of this love, the worse the people.[5] By our definition, the Roman people is a people and its estate is without doubt a commonwealth. As for the objects of that people's love, both in its earliest days and in later periods, and that people's morality, moving from bloody partisan strife, to social and civil wars, corrupting and disrupting the very unity that is the health of a people: for all this we have the witness of history, and I have had a great deal to say about it in my preceding books. Yet I will not make that a reason for asserting that a people is not really a people or that a state is not a commonwealth, so long as there remains an association of some kind or other between a multitude of rational beings united by a common agreement on the objects of its love.[6]

City of God XIX.24

Without justice, what are kingdoms but gangs of criminals on a large scale?[7] What are criminal gangs but petty kingdoms? A gang is a group under the command of a leader, held together by a pact of association. They divide their plunder according to agreed-upon rules.

If villains like these win so many recruits from the ranks of the demoralized that they acquire territory, establish a base, capture cities,

8 Here Augustine applies what he considers Christian virtues to the office and task of governing. He has in mind several Christian Roman emperors who brought integrity to their role and who also helped the spread of Christianity. However, his description of a good ruler in this paragraph can be generalized to any time or place.

9 This line refers to his own church. Augustine always pushes beyond social role or position to deeper motivation. People have all sorts of reasons for being Christian—many of which have nothing to do with Christ. And many people who are not "one of us" in the church, says Augustine, may live in the love and justice that Christ taught. God's grace and human choice are not bound by the limits of social categories or institutions. That is why the City of God is not coextensive with the Christian Church or with any religion.

Augustine always maintains the mystery and ambiguity of human motivation, so he believes we should not judge whether others are citizens of the City of God or the City of Man. Some days we can hardly discern the depths of our own motivations for the choices we make.

and subdue peoples, then they call themselves a kingdom. So in the eyes of the world, they become a kingdom, not by renouncing aggression, but by attaining impunity.

A captured pirate gave a quick and cutting response to Alexander the Great. The king asked him, "What is your idea, infesting the sea?" The pirate answered with uninhibited insolence: "The same as yours, infesting the earth! But because I do it with a small ship, I'm called a pirate. Because you do it with a navy, you're called an emperor!"

CITY OF GOD IV.4

We Christians call rulers happy if they rule with justice, if amid the voices of high praise and reverential greetings of excessive humility, they are not puffed up with pride, but remember they are only men; if they put their power at the service of God's majesty and spread God's worship far and wide; if they fear, love, and worship God; if, more than their earthly kingdom, they love that realm where they are not afraid to share the kingship; if they are slow to punish, but ready to pardon; if they take vengeance on wrong because of the need to lead and protect the state, and not to satisfy personal animosity; if they grant pardon not to allow impunity for wrongdoing, but in hopes that the wrongdoer will make amends; if when they must make severe decisions, as often happens, they balance this with gentle mercy and generous benefit; if they restrain their own self-indulgent appetites even more because they are free to gratify them, and prefer command over their lower desires than over any number of subject peoples; and if they do all this not out of a burning desire for hollow praise, but for the love of eternal happiness; and if they do not fail to give the true God the offering of humility, compassion, and prayer as a sacrifice for their sins.[8]

CITY OF GOD XIX.24

Many who seem outside are really inside, and many who seem inside are really outside.[9]

EXPOSITIONS OF THE PSALMS 106.14

For Augustine, justice in human affairs is rooted in respect for what he understood as the hierarchy of created beings. Like other ancient philosophers and theologians, Augustine believed spiritual realities were superior to material ones. All things are good, because all things come from God the Creator. But there is a hierarchy of goods, ascending from inanimate matter like rocks, to the living matter of plants, to living animals, to human beings who are rational animals with souls, to the angels who are rational spiritual beings, to God who is infinite Spirit.

Justice means observing this order of created beings. We should treat every created being with the respect due to its place in the universe. This means that lower things are to be subjected to higher things: a human child is more important than a pet. A living pet is more important than a "pet rock." It also means—and herein lies the foundation of Augustine's principle of social justice—that equality must be preserved among things that are equal. All human beings, because they are of the same order of creation, are to be treated equally.

1 This passage summarizes the dynamic of moral or ethical living as Augustine understands it: to distinguish the relative orders of creation, to examine and weigh the various options for action before us, and to choose in ways that subordinate lesser goods to greater ones, and in ways that honor the equality among members of the same order. *Letter* 140 is very long—Augustine refers to it as a book. He wrote it around 411 or 412, around the same time he was beginning to formulate ideas for *City of God*, and as refugees were pouring into North Africa from Italy. Amidst the political instability of the time, Augustine was formulating principles of order that helped establish justice amidst social disruption.

□ Justice

As all the things that God created are good, from the rational creature itself to the lowest body, so the rational soul acts well in these if it preserves order and, by distinguishing, choosing, and weighing well, subordinates lesser goods to greater ones, bodily ones to spiritual ones, inferior ones to superior ones, temporal ones to everlasting ones.... Since all substances are naturally good, praiseworthy order is honored in them, and blameworthy disorder is condemned.[1]

LETTER 140.4

A true Christian should never set himself up over other human beings.... If you wish to be better than another person, you will grudge to see that person as your equal. Therefore, you ought to wish all equal to yourself.

HOMILIES ON THE FIRST EPISTLE OF JOHN 8.8

2 This passage comes from a letter Augustine wrote around 423 or 424 to his lifelong friend Alypius. Alypius, like Augustine, became a Christian and eventually a bishop in Africa. This letter, which had been lost for centuries, was discovered in a library in Vienna in 1981. It shows how Augustine dealt with the serious problem of women and children being kidnapped and sold into slavery. Here is the great theologian discussing with a dear friend his concerns over one of the great injustices that confronted him as a pastor. Sadly, the North African slave trade of the fifth century described by Augustine in this letter could be mistaken for an account of similar atrocities of the West African–American slave trade of the sixteenth- to nineteenth-centuries, and of the continuing market of human beings across international borders today.

3 Many free citizens who were landowners were so heavily taxed they had to resort to selling their children into service until their twenty-fifth year. This was legal, according to Roman law. In the Roman Empire, and in the ancient world in general, slavery was an accepted social reality. In North Africa, almost every household of some means would have at least one man slave and one woman slave who were generally well treated and considered part of the household. In *Confessions*, Augustine mentions the servant girl who tattled on Monica when she was a teenager for tasting too much wine in the cellar (*Confessions* IX.8.18). Augustine himself would have been accompanied to school in his early years by the family's manservant.

These household slaves would have enjoyed a lifestyle more comfortable and secure than that of their poor, tax-burdened parents, who were forced to mortgage their own children. So while Augustine considers slavery an unnatural social status that violates the order of creation, he accepts it as one result of original sin and counsels that all members of a household, slave or free, should be treated with equal respect (*City of God* XIX.14,15,16). The violent kidnapping and selling of innocents, however, is a totally different matter that violates all social order.

There is in Africa such a great multitude of men who are commonly called slave merchants that they seem to drain this land to a large extent of its human population by transferring those whom they buy—almost all of them freemen—to the provinces overseas.[2] For scarcely a few are found to have been sold by their parents, and they do not buy these, as the laws of Rome allow, for work lasting twenty-five years, but they buy them precisely as slaves and sell them overseas as slaves.[3] But only most rarely do they buy true slaves from their masters. Now from this multitude of merchants a multitude of trappers and raiders has grown so great that it is reported that they invade certain remote and rural sites, where the population is small, in shrieking mobs with the terrifying apparel of either soldiers or barbarians, and they sell to these merchants those whom they carry off by violence....

4 Alypius was traveling in Italy when Augustine sent him this letter. Even in Italy, this African horror of kidnapping innocents for slavery was well known.

Later in this same letter, Augustine describes how, while he himself was away from Hippo, his congregation rescued almost one hundred and twenty people who had been kidnapped and were being held in Hippo for transport overseas. The congregation put up money to ransom the slaves and thereby secured their release so they could return to their villages and families.

5 A number of medieval manuscripts containing forgotten letters of Augustine were discovered in the 70s and 80s and were inserted into the existing corpus of letters. *Letter* 10.2, 3 is one of these letters.

6 Augustine is commenting on day three of the creation story in the book of Genesis. God commands the earth to bear fruit. Augustine spins out a spiritual or metaphorical interpretation of this text. He believes that God's command to bear fruit also applies to us as human beings. The particular way in which we are to "fructify" is by works of justice and charity toward each other. Thus, Augustine roots his theology of justice in the very beginning of the Bible as part of divine creation. In fact, divine creation is ongoing. God's work of bringing forth the orders of creation, described in Genesis, is a continuing reality. Through human works of justice, God continues to bring forth created order in the world. For Augustine, this is a central truth about the nature of creation and of our role in it.

In a tiny village, women and children were carried off to be sold after the men had been killed through such attacks.... I myself asked a certain girl from among those who, through our church, were set free from this wretched captivity how she was sold to the slave merchants. She said that she was seized from her parents' house. Then I asked whether she was the only one who had been there, and she answered that this happened when her parents and brothers were present. Her brother, who had come to take her back, was also there, and because she was little, he explained how it had come about. He said that these raiders had broken in at night and that the family hid themselves from them as best they could rather than venture to resist them, since they believed that they were barbarians. But if there were no slave merchants, those things would not happen. And I certainly do not think that rumor is silent about this evil in Africa, even where you are.[4]

LETTER 10.2, 3[5]

We fructify [bear fruit] in love of our neighbors by assisting them in their bodily needs, for, having seed of similar kind within ourselves, we learn by compassion from our own weakness.[6] So we are impelled to succor the needy in the way we would wish to be relieved ourselves, were we in the same distress. This means not only the easy provision that could be likened to seed-bearing grass; we may also be called upon to supply the stout, oaklike protection of a fruit-bearing tree, which in its benign strength can lift an injured person clear of the grasp of a powerful oppressor, and furnish protective shade by the unshakable firmness of just judgment.

And so I pray you, Lord: as you cause joy and strength to spring and grow, even so let the truth spring up: let it sprout from the earth, and let righteousness look down from heaven, and let luminaries be set in the firmament. Let us break our bread for the hungry and bring the homeless poor under our roof, let us clothe the naked and not spurn our own kin. When these fruits are burgeoning on earth, take heed and see that it is good. Then may swift dawn break for us, so that rising from

6 Augustine's ideas about social justice are clear. He is what today might be called a "redistributionist" in his political-social theory. He does not support any absolute right to private property, either land or wealth. Because all human beings are equal, the rights and needs of all are superior to any individual amassing of wealth or power that ignores those in need.

Augustine's idea of a just society is evident in his monastic rule. He directs monks and nuns to live in community where all things are held in common and each member receives according to his or her need. He finds support for this radical way of living in the New Testament Book called the Acts of the Apostles (Acts 2:44–47).

7 The date of this sermon is around 410 or 411. He is probably referring to the sack of Rome by Alaric in August 410 when he says elsewhere in the sermon: "How many people, after all, have suddenly lost all their possessions at a stroke, after hoarding them so carefully! One incursion of the enemy, and all the savings of the wealthy were lost." He must have watched as refugees from Rome landed at the port of Hippo, unloading what they were able to save as they fled Rome and paying porters at the wharf to help them with their burdens.

The dislocation and dispossession suffered by the exiles from Italy were not only an occasion for Augustine's congregation to help these refugees, but also a reminder not to hoard goods.

this lowly crop of active works to the delights of contemplation, we may lay hold on the Word of Life above and appear like luminaries for the world, firmly set in the vault that is your scripture.

Confessions XIII.17.21; 18.22

God does not demand much of you. He asks back what he gave you, and from him you take what is enough for you. The superfluities of the rich are the necessities of the poor. When you possess superfluities, you possess what belongs to others.[6]

Expositions of the Psalms 147.12

Do you think it's a small matter that you are eating someone else's food? Listen to the apostle; we brought nothing into this world, yet a full table is spread before you. The earth and its fullness belong to God [not to the powerful, wealthy individuals or nations]. God bestows the world on the poor; God bestows it on the rich.

Sermon 29.2–4

What are the poor people we give charity to, but our porters, whom we hire to transfer our assets from earth to heaven? You give the stuff to your porter; he carries what you give him to heaven. "How," you say, "does he carry it to heaven? Look, I see him spending it all on food."

But that's just it; it's by spending it on food, not by keeping it, that he transports it. Or has this slipped your mind: *Come, you blessed of my Father, take possession of the kingdom. For I was hungry and you gave me to eat* (Matthew 25:34–35)?... Christ has received what you have given; it has been received by the one who gave you the means to give it; it has been received by the one who at the end will give you himself.[7]

Sermon 389.4

8 This passage reveals how deeply Augustine thought about social justice and charity. The goal of such good works is not to reinforce social structures that keep certain members of society in want and need. The goal of justice is found in the root of justice: complete human equality that is to be expressed in and protected by appropriate social structures and institutions. Moral behavior requires a constant vigilance about motivation for ethical choices.

For we mustn't wish that there be unfortunates, so that we may be able to exercise the works of mercy. You give bread to the hungry, but it would be better if no one were hungry and you gave to no one. You clothe the naked. Would that all were clothed and there weren't this need! You bury the dead. Would that that life would finally come in which no one dies! You bring concord to those who are quarreling. Would that there would finally be that eternal peace of Jerusalem, where no one is in discord! For all of these are the duties of necessity. Take away the unfortunates, and the works of mercy will cease. The works of mercy will cease; will the warmth of charity be extinguished? You love with more genuineness a well-off person to whom you have nothing to offer. That love will be purer and much more sincere. For, if you have made an offering to an unfortunate, perhaps you desire to extol yourself over him, and you want him—who is the author of your good deed—to be subject to you. He was needy, you bestowed something. You seem greater, because you made the offering, than him to whom the offering was made. Choose to be equal, so that both of you may be under the one to whom nothing can be offered.[8]

HOMILIES ON THE FIRST EPISTLE OF JOHN 8.5

One of Augustine's enduring legacies is his so-called theory of just war. His reflections on the horrors of war are counterbalanced by his conviction that sometimes war is necessary. However, he is clear that war is just only under certain conditions. It should be declared only to maintain or reestablish justice, that is, the right treatment of people in society. Only a duly recognized leader can make the decision to go to war to restore justice in society. During the execution of a war, all means must be taken to avoid unneeded and excessive force. The only right outcome of war is a peace that respects justice, even for the vanquished, and that cultivates a society that promotes what is best in people.

Presidents George W. Bush and Barack Obama have appealed to these elements of just war in their arguments for waging war against terrorism in Iraq and Afghanistan.

1 The "earthly city," or City of Man, as we have seen, is Augustine's language for individuals and societies characterized by selfishness and self-centeredness. It denotes persons who make decisions solely to advance their own aims, no matter the expense or harm to others, to social structures, or to the environment. Such selfishness can come to epitomize a state or society that sacrifices the common good to increase the wealth or power of its dominant group or class. Such a state, should it ever declare war, is much less likely to secure true peace. So, by Augustine's standards, such a state is not likely to prosecute a just war.

2 Augustine presents his basic argument for going to war: the defeat of injustice. This is what comes to be known in just war theory as the *jus belli*, that is, the right reason for the conduct of war.

□ War

The human race populated the whole earth. Though spread across a wide variety of geographical locations, human beings were still linked together by a kind of fellowship based on a common nature, though each group pursued its own advantage and sought to fulfill its own desires. In such pursuits not everyone, perhaps no one, is completely satisfied, because people have conflicting goals. So human society is generally divided against itself, and one part, finding itself stronger, oppresses another. The conquered then submit to the conqueror, naturally choosing peace and survival at any price, so that it astonishes us when people prefer death to slavery.

CITY OF GOD XVIII.2

The earthly city is mostly divided against itself by legal conflicts, by wars, by battles, by the pursuit of victories that bring death with them or at best are doomed to death. If any part of the earthly city rises up in war against another part, it seeks victory over other nations, though it itself is enslaved to its own base passions. If in victory it exalts in arrogance, such victory brings death in its wake.... Such victory is doomed to death.[1]

CITY OF GOD XV.4

War is always unfortunate. But it is more unfortunate when the unjust triumph over the just. Good people can consider the necessity of going to war to prevent the triumph of the unjust as a blessed course of action.[2]

CITY OF GOD IV.14

3 The wise man or woman is a reference to the Wisdom literature of the Hebrew Bible. That literature praises the person who seeks to live by God's commands and counsels. No such person ever takes delight in war and chooses it only with great reluctance.

4 According to Augustine, for a war to be just it is not enough that its goal be the restoration of justice. Those who wage a just war must constantly examine their motivation and monitor their lust for power and dominance, as well as their hatred for the enemy. Augustine, an experienced observer of human behavior and its motives, is knowingly setting very high standards for a just war.

This concern for the practice of the principles of justice during war is called *jus in bello*.

A wise man wages a just war. As a human being, he certainly regrets the fact that he must wage a just war. If all wars were unjust, he would never have to go to war, so there would never be war for the wise man. It is the injustice of the opposing side that imposes on the wise man the duty of waging war. As a human being, he finds this injustice deplorable—the injustice of other human beings—and only reluctantly goes to war against it. Sadly, everyone who knows the evils of war, its horror and cruelty, must acknowledge the misery it entails. Anyone who experiences such evils, or even thinks about them without heartfelt grief is the more to be pitied. He must have lost all human feeling.[3]

CITY OF GOD XIX.7

The desire to do harm, cruelty in taking vengeance, a mind that is without peace and incapable of peace, fierceness in rebellion, the lust for domination, and anything else of the sort—these are the things that are rightly blamed in wars ... not human beings, who die so that others will be subdued and live in peace.[4]

ANSWER TO FAUSTUS, A MANICHEAN 22.74

5   Augustine wrote this letter around 411 or 412 to Marcellinus, imperial commissioner in Africa. He assures his Christian friend and soldier
that Christ is not opposed to all forms of war. At the same time, he
proposes a high standard of behavior and morals for the military. The
bishop counsels his young friend that the true soldier conquers evil in
himself and conquers others only so that the former enemy will have
the benefit of a new society in which he or she can likewise overcome
the evil tendencies that arise from concupiscence as a result of original
sin. Tragically, Marcellinus himself was put to death by the injustice of
the Roman state, much to Augustine's dismay.

6   Once peace is achieved, a society must be vigilant in its defense of
justice. This is called *jus post bello*, justice after war.

7   Augustine wrote these astonishing words in a letter to a friend who
had asked for clarification on some moral issues. Augustine does not
approve of vigilante killing in self-defense—only in the case of a soldier fighting in a just war. The soldier's role in war is to fight for the
restoration of justice.

We must, then, always keep those precepts of patience in the disposition of the heart, and we must always have benevolence in the will so that we do not return evil for evil. But we also have to do many things, even against the will of people who need to be punished with a certain kind harshness, for we have to consider their benefit rather than their will ... for in rebuking a child, no matter how harshly, a father's love is surely never lost; he nonetheless does what the son does not want and causes pain to the son who, despite his unwillingness, he judges must be healed by pain. And for this reason, if this earthly state keeps the Christian commandments, even wars will not be waged without goodwill in order more easily to take into account the interests of the conquered with a view to a society made peaceful with piety and justice. For a person whose freedom for wickedness is taken away is conquered to his own benefit, because nothing is more unhappy than the happiness of sinners that nourishes their penal impunity and strengthens their evil will like an internal enemy.[5]

LETTER 138.2.14

If victory is won by those fighting for the more just cause, then that victory is undoubtedly a cause for rejoicing. The resulting peace is something to be desired. These things are good and surely gifts of God. But if the higher goods proper to the City of God are neglected (goods that lead ultimately to perfect, everlasting peace), if these higher goods are neglected and only earthly goods are considered or preferred to higher goods, then the unavoidable consequence will be new trouble and growing unhappiness.[6]

CITY OF GOD XV.4

I do not approve of the advice about killing human beings for fear that one might be killed by them, unless one is perhaps a soldier or is obligated by public office so that he does this, not for himself, but for others or for the city where he himself also lives, after he has received lawful authority, if it is appropriate to his person.[7]

LETTER 47.5

8 Augustine's argument for social order is so strong and pervasive that he justifies the soldier forced to fight for an unjust king. Even if the war itself is not just, the need for social order requires the soldier to obey. Augustine was not generally supportive of civil rebellion. He thought it overturned the social order without necessarily restoring justice—at least that was the repeated history of Rome.

9 Augustine provides an ancient expression of what will become known in Islam as the *jihad*: the war of conquest over the evil that is in a person's heart. As Augustine sees it, God arms us for this victory over evil within. If we were to rely on our own defenses, we would ultimately be conquered by this evil. It is through divine grace that we gain strength to win this internal war.

It makes a difference for which causes and under what authority people undertake the waging of war. But the natural order that aims at the peace of mortals demand that the authority and the decision to undertake war rest with the ruler, while soldiers have the duty of carrying out the commands of war for the common peace and security…. If, therefore, a just man is perhaps serving as a soldier under a godless human king, he can correctly fight at his command so as to preserve the order of civil peace.[8] This is certain when what is commanded is not against the commandment of God or when it is not certain whether it is or is not. In the latter case, the injustice in commanding perhaps makes the king guilty, but his order in obeying proves the soldier innocent. How much more is he who wages war at God's command completely innocent in the conduct of wars!

ANSWER TO FAUSTUS, A MANICHEAN 22.75

If God takes up our cause, will he abandon us in our unarmed condition? By no means. He equips us, but with weapons of a different order, the evangelical weapons of truth, self-control, salvation, hope, faith, and charity. We shall wield these weapons, but they will not come from ourselves. The arms we did have as from ourselves will have been burnt, provided that we are enkindled by that fire of the Holy Spirit of which the psalm declares, *The shields he will burn with fire.* You aspired to be more powerful in yourself, but God has made you weak in order to make you strong with his strength, for your own was nothing but weakness.[9]

EXPOSITIONS OF THE PSALMS 45.13

◥ The word "restless" describes so much of Augustine's life. As a young man he was restless in his search for truth: "You have made us for yourself, O Lord, and our heart is unquiet until it rests in you." Even after his conversion to Christianity, Augustine remains restless, unquiet in his continuing search for ever deeper understandings of God, of love, of faith, of others, of life itself.

Yet he counsels peace. Augustine teaches that by discovering and respecting the created order of the universe, by loving things and people and God in proportion to their value in the hierarchy of being, a person can experience a foretaste of the peace that will be ours in eternal union with God. In this life, our weakness and concupiscence interferes with our desire to love in an ordered way. Yet by grace we come to know how to love; by grace we are strengthened to love. For Augustine, grace leads us to peace, both to the measure of peace we might experience in this life and to the perfect peace of eternal life.

1 Augustine's idea of ordered loving should not be confused with restrictive living. Restraint and respect in loving is not the same as repressed or suppressed loving. Augustine was a man of great passion and strong emotion. The North African culture in which he lived was known around the Roman Empire for the depth of its ardor and feeling. For Augustine, love is the most powerful force in human nature, a trace element of our divine origin. He is convinced that love grows stronger and more powerful when it is properly focused and creatively channeled. The power of love, like the power of nuclear reaction, needs to be contained and directed to achieve its greatest potential. Peace is not an emotionally vapid tranquility marked with a "do not disturb" sign. Peace is love pulsing through all our relationships in ways that reflect the differences and respect the diversity of creation.

□ Peace

Peace is the tranquility of order.... Peace in our body comes when all its parts are working together in an orderly balance. Peace in the appetites of our irrational soul comes when we control their satisfaction. Peace in our rational soul comes when we act in accord with our convictions. Peace between body and soul comes when the soul respectfully and healthily rules the body. Peace between a human being and God comes from an ordered obedience based on faith. Peace among persons comes from ordered agreement. Peace in the home comes from the ordered harmony of authority and obedience among those who live there. The peace of the Heavenly City lies in a perfectly ordered and harmonious relationship among those who find their joy in God and each other in God. The peace of the whole universe is the tranquility of order. And order is the arrangement of like and unlike things in their proper place.[1]

City of God XIX.13

The delight of peace is so great that even on the level of earthly and temporal values, no word is more welcome to our ears, nothing is more desirable, nothing is better than peace.... Just as there is no one who does not wish for joy, so there is no one who does not wish for peace. Even when people choose war, they wish for victory, they fight for peace with glory.

City of God XIX.11, 12

2 Concupiscence of lust, of pointless curiosity, and of power often compromise our ability to love properly.

3 The eventuality of death will always to some extent compromise our experience of peace on this earth.

4 This is again Augustine's idea of divinization, his teaching that through the enlightenment and empowerment of divine grace human beings become more and more like God, sharing more and more in the divine nature.

5 Augustine's position is that the church, or any people of goodwill, should promote the tranquility of order in whatever society they find themselves. Justice and order provide the members of a society with the opportunity to practice their religious faith and to promote inner peace. He believes that whenever possible the "two cities" should live in peace and make the compromises necessary to achieve and maintain peace. He had studied the tumult of Roman history and seen firsthand the civil and social strife of his own day. He teaches that the fragile peace of civil society should be safeguarded as much as possible.

Augustine does not advocate the establishment of a theocracy based on his Christian views—though later interpreters and critics suggest he does. His understanding of wounded human nature prevents him from idealizing any kind of human society, political or religious. He is too suspect of human motivation and the power of concupiscence to believe that a theocratic state, even a Christian one, would guarantee permanent peace.

What is peace? The absence of war. A state of affairs where there is no strife, no resistance, no adversity. Consider now: are we in that state yet, have we left behind all conflict?... What kind of peace is this, then, which we experience in the teeth of such fierce resistance from vexations, cravings, wants, and weariness? This is no true peace, no perfect peace.[2] When will peace be perfect? *This corruptible body must put on incorruption, and this mortal body be clothed in immortality; then the saying will come true: Death is swallowed up into victory. Where, O death, is your sting: Where is your strife, O death?* (1 Corinthians 15:53–55).[3] From death comes that lassitude we experience in everything that sustains us.... We cannot help desiring that city, whence no friend departs, where no enemy gains entrance, where there is no tempter, no disturber of the peace, no one to cause divisions within God's people, none to collude with the devil in harassing the church, when the prince of demons is flung into eternal fire, along with all those who support him and refuse to abandon his service. A peace made pure will reign among God's children: they will all love themselves as they see themselves full of God, and God will be all in all.[4] For all of us, God will be the object of our contemplation: he will be our common possession, he our common peace. Whatever he gives us now, he himself will be for us then in place of what he gives. He himself will be our peace, perfect and total.

EXPOSITIONS OF THE PSALMS 84.10

The earthly city, whose life is not based on faith, aims at earthly peace. It marks the limits of civil concord by making and keeping laws that establish compromise among human wills regarding those things relevant to our life on earth. By contrast, the Heavenly City, or that part of it which is still living by faith on pilgrimage in our mortal condition, needs this peace until this mortal life—for which earthly peace is essential—passes away.... So it does not hesitate to obey the laws of the earthly city designed for the support of our life on earth. It does this since both cities share in this mortal condition and so that harmony may be preserved between them in this life.[5]

CITY OF GOD XIX.17

6 For Augustine, both justice and peace are achieved through respect for the inherent order of creation. As we have seen previously in the chapter on justice (pages 177–185), Augustine teaches that we are called and empowered by God's grace to love all things and persons according to their proper place in the hierarchy of God's creation. Such ordered loving establishes justice and thereby leads to peace.

7 Augustine often addresses his congregation with this charming title, which calls to mind his theology of grace.

8 The suggestive image of peace as a mistress whose couch one shares is interesting. Was Bishop Augustine remembering his earlier years when his love was less ordered and his life less peaceful?

If you do not love justice, you will not have peace, for these two, justice and peace, love each other, and they embrace, so that anyone who does justice finds peace kissing justice. They are friends, these two; you may perhaps want one without practicing the other, for there is no one who does not want peace, though not everyone wants to act justly. Put the question to all: "Do you want peace?" The entire human race will answer you with a single voice, "I hope for it, I long for it, I want it, I love it." Love justice as well, then, for justice and peace are two friends, kissing each other, and if you do not love peace's friend, peace will not love you or come to you. After all, what is so special about the desire for peace? Every bad person desires peace, for peace is a good thing. But deal justly, because justice and peace kiss each other; there is no quarrel between them.[6]

EXPOSITIONS OF THE PSALMS 84.12

This is the time to encourage your graces,[7] with all the strength God grants me, to love peace, and to pray to the Lord for peace. So let peace be our beloved and our mistress, our hearts be the chaste couch we share with her, enjoying together a quiet mutual trust, and not an association of bitter wrangling, in the loving relationship of inseparable friends.[8]...

[Peace] doesn't make you jealous of anyone who possesses it with you.... Love peace, have peace, be in possession of peace, take to yourself as many others as you can to be in possession of peace with you. The more people it is possessed by, the more extensive it will be. An earthly house hasn't got room for many; the property that is peace grows ever bigger the more inhabitants it has.

SERMON 357.1

9 These paragraphs come at the very end of *Confessions*. In Book XIII, Augustine invites his reader to many levels of interpretation of the first chapter of the book of Genesis. He associates the theme of peace with Sabbath, the seventh and final day of Creation, which has no end.

It's a good thing to love peace, and loving it is having it. Just think how much it is worth! What voice would suffice to praise this saying, what heart to reflect on it: "To love peace is to have it."

So just how much must it be worth, when you have something the moment you love it?... Look, just stay where you are, love peace, and what you love is right there with you. It's a thing of the heart. Nor do you share peace with your friends in the same way as you share bread. If you want to share bread, of course, the more people you break it to, the less there is left where that came from. Peace, though, is like that bread that increased in the hands of the Lord's disciples as they broke and distributed it.

Be at peace therefore, brothers and sisters, with each other. If you want to draw others to peace, you must first have it yourselves, first hold onto it yourselves. Let what you have glow in you, so as to kindle others.

SERMON 357.2, 3

Give us peace, Lord God, for you have given us all else; give us the peace that is repose, the peace of the Sabbath, and the peace that knows no evening. This whole order of exceedingly good things, intensely beautiful as it is, will pass away when it has served its purpose: these things too will have their morning and their evening.[9]

But the seventh day has no evening and sinks toward no sunset, for you sanctified it that it might abide forever. After completing your exceedingly good works, you rested on the seventh day, though you achieved them in repose; and you willed your book to tell us this as a promise that when our works are finished (works exceedingly good inasmuch as they are your gift to us), we too may rest in you, the Sabbath of eternal life.

CONFESSIONS XIII.35.50–36.51

As a Christian, Augustine believed that at death "life is not ended but changed" (eucharistic prayer from the Roman liturgy). He believed in the resurrection of the dead and life everlasting. Augustine understood eternal life to be a sharing in the life of the Trinity Itself.

Yet, he also reflects on the painful reality of death. There are few more moving passages in Latin literature than the narrative in Book IX of *Confessions* that recounts the death of his mother, Monica. And as Possidius recounts in his *Life of Saint Augustine*, Augustine prepared for his own death consciously and prayerfully.

1 Augustine is fascinated with the notion of time. In *Confessions*, he writes: "What, then, is time? If no one asks me, I know; if I want to explain it to someone who asks me, I do not know" (XI.14.17). He continues analyzing the nature of time for several pages, reaching the conclusion that even the smallest conceivable microsecond is itself divisible into past and future. "Hence the present is reduced to vanishing-point" (*Confessions* XI.15.20). As quickly as realities come from the future into the experience that we call the present, they fade into the past. Time is the all-pervasive evidence of our mortality and of the contingency of all creation. Only God is eternal. For Augustine, we pass out of time through death into the endless Sabbath of God's eternity.

☐ Death

You know how we commonly say, "This year ..."; but how much of this year do we have in our grasp, except the current day? The earlier days of this year have passed already, and we cannot hold onto them; while the future days have not yet come. We are living in one day only, yet we say, "This year." You ought to say, "Today," if you want to indicate what is present; for what do you hold as present out of this whole year? The part of it that has passed exists no longer, and the part of it that is still to come does not exist yet. So how can you say, "This year"? Speak more accurately; say, "Today." Yes, you reply, you are right. I will henceforth say, "Today."

But you still need to pay attention to your language, because the early morning hours have already passed, while the later hours have not yet arrived. Correct your mode of speech then; say, "This hour." But how much of this hour is within your grasp? Some of its seconds have already flown by, and those still left have not yet come. Say, "This moment," then. But what moment? It is gone even while I am pronouncing its syllables! Look: two syllables, "mo-ment." The second is not audible until the first has died away. Even if we take a single syllable, a syllable composed of two letters, the second letter cannot make itself heard until the first has faded. What, then, can we hold onto of our years?[1] These years are subject to change. We must focus our thoughts on the years of eternity, the years that are stable, the years that are not a succession of days that arrive and pass away, the years of which scripture says to God in another text, *You are the selfsame, and your years will not fail* (Psalm 101:28 [102:27]).

EXPOSITIONS OF THE PSALMS 76.8

2 These passages recount in touching detail Monica's death and Augustine's emotional response.

3 Augustine; his mother, Monica; his brother, Navigius; his son, Adeodatus; and other family and friends were on their way back to Africa. Augustine had resigned his imperial post in the autumn of 386 and was baptized at Milan together with his son and his friend Alypius in April 387. Having traveled from Milan south to Rome, they were now stuck in Ostia, Rome's port city at the mouth of the Tiber River, which was under a military blockade. There in temporary quarters, in the autumn of 387, Monica died, probably of malaria, which was endemic in the marshy lands around the river.

The theme of pilgrimage suggests itself here. The small band of Africans was en route back home—Monica was not to make it. Her pilgrimage of faith was to end here, in a foreign land, which was to become for her the gate, the opening or mouth (*ostia*) of heaven.

4 A reference to the eucharistic liturgy celebrated in her memory. Today, this practice of celebrating Mass in memory of the deceased remains part of Catholic tradition and practice.

5 He would have been about fourteen or fifteen years old.

My mother took to her bed with fever.**2** One day during her illness she lapsed into unconsciousness and for a short time was unaware of her surroundings. We all came running, but she quickly returned to her senses, and, gazing at me and my brother as we stood there, she asked in puzzlement, "Where was I?" We were bewildered with grief, but she looked keenly at us and said, "You are to bury your mother here." I was silent, holding back my tears, but my brother said something about his hope that she would not die far from home, but in her own country, for that would be a happier way.**3** On hearing this, she looked anxious and her eyes rebuked him for thinking so; then she turned her gaze from him to me and said, "What silly talk!" Not long afterward, addressing us both, she said, "Lay this body anywhere, and take no trouble over it. One thing only do I ask of you, that you remember me at the altar of the Lord wherever you may be."**4** Having made her meaning clear to us with such words as she could muster, she fell silent, and travailed as the disease grew worse....

On the ninth day of her illness, in the fifty-sixth year of her age, in my thirty-third year, that religious and godly soul was set free from her body.

I closed her eyes, and a huge sadness surged into my heart; the tears welled up, but in response to a ferocious command from my mind, my eyes held the fount in check until it dried up, though the struggle was intensely painful for me. But as she breathed her last, the boy Adeodatus burst out crying;**5** he was restrained by all of us and grew quiet. By this means something boyish in myself, which was sliding toward tears, was also restrained by the man's voice of my heart, and it too grew quiet....

Little by little, I recovered my earlier thoughts about your handmaid, remembering how devout had been her attitude toward you, and how full of holy kindness, how willing to make allowances, she had been in our regard; and now that I was suddenly bereft of this, I found comfort in weeping before you about her and for her, about myself and

6 Augustine's father, Patricius, became a Christian before he died. Earlier in *Confessions*, Augustine describes his father as "outstandingly generous, but also hot tempered." He was also regularly unfaithful to Monica. Her patience, however, won him over in the end to her faith.

Augustine writes nothing about the death of his father, which occurred in 372 during Augustine's student years in Carthage. Nor does he mention any details about the death of Adeodatus—perhaps it was too painful to recall. The boy died within a year or two of their return to Africa. So between 386 and 390, Augustine is separated from Adeodatus's mother and loses his own mother and son.

7 Augustine is commenting on the images that the psalmist uses to describe heaven. The powerful analogy of being "drunk on God" gives Augustine the opportunity to suggest that our relationship with God in the next life will be so powerful as almost to extinguish our individual minds as we are pulled into and transformed by divinity itself. The word "almost" is theologically important. In Eastern religion, the individuality of the person vanishes into the Eternal Oneness of the Godhead. In Augustine's theology, the infinite love of God transforms but does not extinguish who we are as persons.

for myself. The tears that I had been holding back I now released to flow as plentifully as they would, and strewed them as a bed beneath my heart....

May she rest in peace with her husband. She was married to no other man either before or after him, and in serving him she brought forth fruit for you by patience, to win him for you in the end.[6] Inspire others, my Lord, my God, inspire your servants who are my brethren, your children who are my masters, whom I now serve with heart and voice and pen, that as many of them as read this may remember Monica, your servant, at your altar, along with Patricius, sometime her husband. From their flesh you brought me into this life, though how I do not know. Let them remember with loving devotion these two who were my parents in this transitory light, but also were my brethren under you, our Father, within our mother the Catholic Church.

Confessions IX.11.27–13.37

The psalmist searched for some expression derived from human experience that he could use to say what he meant [by seeing God face to face]. He saw people immersing themselves in drunkenness, taking too much wine and losing their senses; then he knew how he must express it, for we have been given a joy beyond all telling. The human mind almost vanishes, becoming in some sense divinized, and is inebriated by the rich abundance of God's house....[7] Water rushing with mighty force is called a torrent. God's mercy will flow with mighty force to water and inebriate those who in this present life fix their hope beneath the shadow of his wings. What is that delight? It is like a torrent that inebriates the thirsty. Let any who are thirsty now fix their hopes there; let the thirsty have hope, because one day, inebriated, they will have the reality. Until they have the reality, let them thirstily hope.

Expositions of the Psalms 35.14

8 Sometime in the decades following Augustine's death, the Vandals, who were Arian Christians, exiled the Catholic bishops of North Africa. During that relocation, Augustine's remains were transferred across the sea to the island of Sardinia. There they remained until the eighth century when they were ransomed by Luitprand, king of the Lombard region of Italy. He brought them to the city of Pavia where they are still venerated in the Augustinian Church of San Pietro in Ciel d'Oro.

God granted this holy man a long life for the benefit and prosperity of his holy church (he lived seventy-six years, almost forty of them as a cleric and bishop).... In order that his recollection might not be broken, about ten days before departing from the body, he asked us who were present not to let anyone in to see him except when the doctors came to examine him or his meals were brought to him. His wish was carefully respected, and he spent the entire time in prayer. Right down to his final illness, he preached the Word of God in the church uninterruptedly, zealously, and courageously, and with soundness of mind and judgment. Then, with all his bodily members still intact and with sight and hearing undiminished, as we stood by watching and praying, he fell asleep with his fathers (as scripture says) in a good old age. A sacrifice was offered to God in our presence to commend his bodily death, and then he was buried.[8]

He did not make a will because as a poor man of God he had nothing to leave. He always intended that the library of the church and all the books in it should be carefully preserved for posterity. From these, thank God, we can know his quality and importance as a churchman; in them he will always be alive for the faithful.... This is certainly acknowledged by those who read his writings on the things of God. I believe, however, that they profited even more who were able to hear him speaking in church and see him there present, especially if they were familiar with his manner of life among his fellow human beings.

THE LIFE OF SAINT AUGUSTINE BY SAINT POSSIDIUS XXXI.1, 3, 5, 6, 9

Suggestions for Further Study ☐

Books

Brown, Peter. *Augustine of Hippo: A Biography*. Berkeley: University of California Press, 2000.

First published in 1967, this work revived contemporary interest in Augustine.

Chadwick, Henry. *Augustine of Hippo: A Life*. New York: Oxford University Press, 2009.

Posthumous publication of Chadwick's lifetime of research and writing.

Fitzgerald, Allan D., ed. *Augustine through the Ages: An Encyclopedia*. Grand Rapids, Mich.: William B. Eerdmans, 1999.

An invaluable compilation of the best of contemporary Augustinian scholarship with five hundred entries by almost one hundred and fifty scholars.

Fredriksen, Paula. *Augustine and the Jews: A Christian Defense of Jews and Judaism*. New York: Doubleday, 2008.

A close, seminal study of Augustine's evolving and original understanding of the relationship between Jews and Christians.

Lancel, Serge. *St. Augustine*. London: SCM Press, 2002.

A masterly overview of Augustine's life, time, and works.

Websites

www.augustinianheritage.org
Information on "The Works of Saint Augustine: A Translation for the 21st Century."

www.augnet.org/default.asp
See "Works of Augustine" tab for a list of Augustine's writings.

www9.georgetown.edu/faculty/jod/augustine/
An overview of resources in Augustinian Studies by James J. O'Donnell of Georgetown University.

www41.homepage.villanova.edu/donald.burt/
Augustinian spirituality and philosophy by Donald X. Burt, OSA, of Villanova University.

www.augustinians.net
  Information about the Order of Saint Augustine worldwide.

Miniseries

Dugay, Christian. *Augustine: The Decline of the Roman Empire.* Rome: Lux Vide, 2009. Miniseries, 200 min.

Available in English as: Dugay, Christian. *The Restless Heart: The Confessions of Saint Augustine.* San Francisco: Ignatius Press, 2012. Film, 127 min.

Index of Texts ☐

Inspiration

Deepening Engagement
Essential Wisdom for Listening and Leading with Purpose, Meaning and Joy
By Diane M. Millis, PhD; Foreword by Rob Lehman
A toolkit for community building as well as a resource for personal growth and small group enrichment.
5 x 7¼, 176 pp, Quality PB, 978-1-59473-584-4 **$14.99**

The Rebirthing of God
Christianity's Struggle for New Beginnings
By John Philip Newell
Drawing on modern prophets from East and West, and using the holy island of Iona as an icon of new beginnings, Celtic poet, peacemaker and scholar John Philip Newell dares us to imagine a new birth from deep within Christianity, a fresh stirring of the Spirit.
6 x 9, 160 pp, HC, 978-1-59473-542-4 **$19.99**

Finding God Beyond Religion: A Guide for Skeptics, Agnostics & Unorthodox Believers Inside & Outside the Church
By Tom Stella; Foreword by The Rev. Canon Marianne Wells Borg
Reinterprets traditional religious teachings central to the Christian faith for people who have outgrown the beliefs and devotional practices that once made sense to them.
6 x 9, 160 pp, Quality PB, 978-1-59473-485-4 **$16.99**

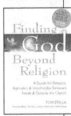

Fully Awake and Truly Alive: Spiritual Practices to Nurture Your Soul
By Rev. Jane E. Vennard; Foreword by Rami Shapiro
Illustrates the joys and frustrations of spiritual practice, offers insights from various religious traditions and provides exercises and meditations to help us become more fully alive.
6 x 9, 208 pp, Quality PB, 978-1-59473-473-1 **$16.99**

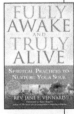

Perennial Wisdom for the Spiritually Independent
Sacred Teachings—Annotated & Explained
Annotation by Rami Shapiro; Foreword by Richard Rohr
Weaves sacred texts and teachings from the world's major religions into a coherent exploration of the five core questions at the heart of every religion's search.
5½ x 8½, 336 pp, Quality PB, 978-1-59473-515-8 **$16.99**

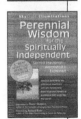

Journeys of Simplicity: Traveling Light with Thomas Merton, Bashō, Edward Abbey, Annie Dillard & Others By Philip Harnden
5 x 7¼, 144 pp, Quality PB, 978-1-59473-181-5 **$12.99**

Saving Civility: 52 Ways to Tame Rude, Crude & Attitude for a Polite Planet
By Sara Hacala 6 x 9, 240 pp, Quality PB, 978-1-59473-314-7 **$16.99**

Spiritually Healthy Divorce: Navigating Disruption with Insight & Hope
By Carolyne Call 6 x 9, 224 pp, Quality PB, 978-1-59473-288-1 **$16.99**

Or phone, mail or email to: SKYLIGHT PATHS Publishing
An imprint of Turner Publishing Company
4507 Charlotte Avenue • Suite 100 • Nashville, Tennessee 37209
Tel: (615) 255-2665 • www.skylightpaths.com
Prices subject to change.

Children's Spirituality

Adam & Eve's First Sunset: God's New Day
By Sandy Eisenberg Sasso; Full-color illus. by Joani Keller Rothenberg
A lesson in hope and faith—and that there are some things beyond our control—for every child who worries about what comes next.
9 x 12, 32 pp, Full-color illus., HC, 978-1-58023-177-0 **$17.95*** For ages 4 & up

Because Nothing Looks Like God
By Lawrence Kushner and Karen Kushner; Full-color illus. by Dawn W. Majewski
Invites parents and children to explore the questions we all have about God.
11 x 8½, 32 pp, Full-color illus., HC, 978-1-58023-092-6 **$18.99*** For ages 4 & up

Also Available: **Teacher's Guide** 8½ x 11, 22 pp, PB, 978-1-58023-140-8 **$6.95**

But God Remembered: Stories of Women from Creation to the Promised Land
By Sandy Eisenberg Sasso; Full-color illus. by Bethanne Andersen
A fascinating collection of four different stories of women only briefly mentioned in biblical tradition and religious texts.
9 x 12, 32 pp, Full-color illus., Quality PB, 978-1-58023-372-9 **$8.99*** For ages 8 & up

Does God Hear My Prayer?
By August Gold; Full-color photos by Diane Hardy Waller
Introduces preschoolers and young readers to prayer and how it helps them express their own emotions.
10 x 8½, 32 pp, Full-color photo illus., Quality PB, 978-1-59473-102-0 **$8.99** For ages 3–6

For Heaven's Sake
By Sandy Eisenberg Sasso; Full-color illus. by Kathryn Kunz Finney
Heaven is often found where you least expect it.
9 x 12, 32 pp, Full-color illus., HC, 978-1-58023-054-4 **$16.95*** For ages 4 & up

In Our Image: God's First Creatures
By Nancy Sohn Swartz God asks all of nature to offer gifts to humankind—with a promise that the humans would care for creation in return.
Full-color illus., eBook, 978-1-58023-520-4 **$16.95*** For ages 5 & up
Animated app available on Apple App Store and The Google Play Marketplace **$9.99**

God's Paintbrush: Special 10th Anniversary Edition
By Sandy Eisenberg Sasso; Full-color illus. by Annette Compton
Invites children of all faiths and backgrounds to encounter God through moments in their own lives.
11 x 8½, 32 pp, Full-color illus., HC, 978-1-58023-195-4 **$17.95*** For ages 4 & up

Also Available: **God's Paintbrush Teacher's Guide**
8½ x 11, 32 pp, PB, 978-1-879045-57-6 **$8.95**

God's Paintbrush Celebration Kit: A Spiritual Activity Kit for Teachers and Students of All Faiths, All Backgrounds 9½ x 12, 40 Full-color Activity Sheets & Teacher Folder w/ complete instructions, HC, 978-1-58023-050-6 **$21.95**
Additional activity sheets available:
8-Student Activity Sheet Pack (40 sheets/5 sessions), 978-1-58023-058-2 **$19.95**
Single-Student Activity Sheet Pack (5 sessions), 978-1-58023-059-9 **$3.95**

Also Available as a Board Book: **I Am God's Paintbrush**
5 x 5, 24 pp, Full-color illus., Board Book, 978-1-59473-265-2 **$7.99** For ages 1–4

It's a ... It's a ... It's a Mitzvah
By Liz Suneby and Diane Heiman; Full-color Illus. by Laurel Molk
A whimsical, fun-filled book that helps parents and young children explore the joys of doing good deeds together.
9 x 12, 32 pp Full-color illus., HC, 978-1-58023-509-9 **$18.99*** For ages 3–6

Also Available as a Board Book: **That's a Mitzvah**
5 x 5, 24 pp, Full-color illus., Board Book, 978-1-58023-804-5 **$8.99*** For ages 1–4

*A book from Jewish Lights, SkyLight Paths' sister imprint

Spiritual Poetry—The Mystic Poets

Experience these mystic poets as you never have before. Each beautiful, compact book includes a brief introduction to the poet's time and place, a summary of the major themes of the poet's mysticism and religious tradition, essential selections from the poet's most important works, and an appreciative preface by a contemporary spiritual writer.

Hafiz
The Mystic Poets
Translated and with Notes by Gertrude Bell
Preface by Ibrahim Gamard

Hafiz is known throughout the world as Persia's greatest poet, with sales of his poems in Iran today only surpassed by those of the Qur'an itself. His probing and joyful verse speaks to people from all backgrounds who long to taste and feel divine love and experience harmony with all living things.
5 x 7¼, 144 pp, HC, 978-1-59473-009-2 **$16.99**

Hopkins
The Mystic Poets
Preface by Rev. Thomas Ryan, CSP

Gerard Manley Hopkins, Christian mystical poet, is beloved for his use of fresh language and startling metaphors to describe the world around him. Although his verse is lovely, beneath the surface lies a searching soul, wrestling with and yearning for God.
5 x 7¼, 112 pp, HC, 978-1-59473-010-8 **$16.99**

Tagore
The Mystic Poets
Preface by Swami Adiswarananda

Rabindranath Tagore is often considered the Shakespeare of modern India. A great mystic, Tagore was the teacher of W. B. Yeats and Robert Frost, the close friend of Albert Einstein and Mahatma Gandhi, and the winner of the Nobel Prize for Literature. This beautiful sampling of Tagore's two most important works, *The Gardener* and *Gitanjali*, offers a glimpse into his spiritual vision that has inspired people around the world.
5 x 7¼, 144 pp, HC, 978-1-59473-008-5 **$16.99**

Whitman
The Mystic Poets
Preface by Gary David Comstock

Walt Whitman was the most innovative and influential poet of the nineteenth century. This beautiful sampling of Whitman's most important poetry from *Leaves of Grass*, and selections from his prose writings, offers a glimpse into the spiritual side of his most radical themes—love for country, love for others and love of self.
5 x 7¼, 192 pp, HC, 978-1-59473-041-2 **$16.99**

Retirement and Later-Life Spirituality

Caresharing
A Reciprocal Approach to Caregiving and Care Receiving in the Complexities of Aging, Illness or Disability
By Marty Richards

Shows how to move from independent to *inter*dependent caregiving, so that the "cared for" and the "carer" share a deep sense of connection.

6 x 9, 256 pp, Quality PB, 978-1-59473-286-7 **$16.99**; HC, 978-1-59473-247-8 **$24.99**

How Did I Get to Be 70 When I'm 35 Inside?
Spiritual Surprises of Later Life
By Linda Douty

Encourages you to focus on the inner changes of aging to help you greet your later years as the grand adventure they can be.

6 x 9, 208 pp, Quality PB, 978-1-59473-297-3 **$16.99**

Soul Fire
Accessing Your Creativity
By Thomas Ryan, CSP

This inspiring guide shows you how to cultivate your creative spirit, particularly in the second half of life, as a way to encourage personal growth, enrich your spiritual life and deepen your communion with God.

6 x 9, 160 pp, Quality PB, 978-1-59473-243-0 **$16.99**

Restoring Life's Missing Pieces
The Spiritual Power of Remembering & Reuniting with People, Places, Things & Self
By Caren Goldman; Foreword by Dr. Nancy Copeland-Payton

Delve deeply into ways that your body, mind and spirit answer the Spirit of Re-union's calls to reconnect with people, places, things and self. A powerful and thought-provoking look at "reunions" of all kinds as roads to remembering the missing pieces of our stories, psyches and souls.

6 x 9, 208 pp, Quality PB, 978-1-59473-295-9 **$16.99**

Creative Aging
Rethinking Retirement and Non-Retirement in a Changing World
By Marjory Zoet Bankson

Explores the spiritual dimensions of retirement and aging and offers creative ways for you to share your gifts and experience, particularly when retirement leaves you questioning who you are when you are no longer defined by your career.

6 x 9, 160 pp, Quality PB, 978-1-59473-281-2 **$16.99**

Creating a Spiritual Retirement
A Guide to the Unseen Possibilities in Our Lives
By Molly Srode

Retirement can be an opportunity to refocus on your soul and deepen the presence of spirit in your life. With fresh spiritual reflections and questions to help you explore this new phase.

6 x 9, 208 pp, b/w photos, Quality PB, 978-1-59473-050-4 **$14.99**

Keeping Spiritual Balance as We Grow Older
More than 65 Creative Ways to Use Purpose, Prayer, and the Power of Spirit to Build a Meaningful Retirement
By Molly and Bernie Srode

As we face new demands on our bodies, it's easy to focus on the physical and forget about the transformations in our spiritual selves. This book is brimming with creative, practical ideas to add purpose and spirit to a meaningful retirement.

8 x 8, 224 pp, Quality PB, 978-1-59473-042-9 **$16.99**

Personal Growth

Deepening Engagement
Essential Wisdom for Listening and Leading with Purpose, Meaning and Joy
By Diane M. Millis, PhD; Foreword by Rob Lehman
A toolkit for community building as well as a resource for personal growth and small group enrichment.
5 x 7¼, 176 pp, Quality PB, 978-1-59473-584-4 **$14.99**

The Forgiveness Handbook
Spiritual Wisdom and Practice for the Journey to Freedom, Healing and Peace
Created by the Editors at SkyLight Paths; Introduction by The Rev. Canon Marianne Wells Borg
Offers inspiration, encouragement and spiritual practice from across faith traditions for all who seek hope, wholeness and the freedom that comes from true forgiveness. 6 x 9, 256 pp, Quality PB, 978-1-59473-577-6 **$18.99**

Decision Making & Spiritual Discernment: The Sacred Art of
Finding Your Way *By Nancy L. Bieber*
Presents three essential aspects of Spirit-led decision making: willingness, attentiveness and responsiveness.
5½ x 8½, 208 pp, Quality PB, 978-1-59473-289-8 **$16.99**

Like a Child
Restoring the Awe, Wonder, Joy and Resiliency of the Human Spirit
By Rev. Timothy J. Mooney
Explores Jesus's counsel to become like children in order to enter the kingdom of God. 6 x 9, 160 pp, Quality PB, 978-1-59473-543-1 **$16.99**

Secrets of a Soulful Marriage
Creating & Sustaining a Loving, Sacred Relationship
By Jim Sharon, EdD, and Ruth Sharon, MS
An innovative, hope-filled resource for developing soulful, mature love for committed couples who are looking to create, maintain and glorify the sacred in their relationship. Offers a banquet of practical tools, inspirational real-life stories and spiritual practices for couples of all faiths, or none.
6 x 9, 192 pp, Quality PB, 978-1-59473-554-7 **$16.99**

A Spirituality for Brokenness
Discovering Your Deepest Self in Difficult Times
By Terry Taylor
Compassionately guides you through the practicalities of facing and finally accepting brokenness in your life—a process that can ultimately bring mending.
6 x 9, 176 pp, Quality PB, 978-1-59473-229-4 **$16.99**

The Bridge to Forgiveness
Stories and Prayers for Finding God and Restoring Wholeness
By Karyn D. Kedar
6 x 9, 176 pp, Quality PB, 978-1-58023-451-1 **$16.99***

Conversation—The Sacred Art
Practicing Presence in an Age of Distraction
By Diane M. Millis, PhD; Foreword by Rev. Tilden Edwards, PhD
5½ x 8½, 192 pp, Quality PB, 978-1-59473-474-8 **$16.99**

Hospitality—The Sacred Art
Discovering the Hidden Spiritual Power of Invitation and Welcome
By Rev. Nanette Sawyer; Foreword by Rev. Dirk Ficca
5½ x 8½, 208 pp, Quality PB, 978-1-59473-228-7 **$16.99**

The Losses of Our Lives
The Sacred Gifts of Renewal in Everyday Loss
By Dr. Nancy Copeland-Payton
6 x 9, 192 pp, Quality PB, 978-1-59473-307-9 **$16.99**; HC, 978-1-59473-271-3 **$19.99**

*A book from Jewish Lights, SkyLight Paths' sister imprint

Women's Interest

There's a Woman in the Pulpit: Christian Clergywomen Share Their Hard Days, Holy Moments & the Healing Power of Humor
Edited by Rev. Martha Spong; Foreword by Rev. Carol Howard Merritt
Offers insight into the lives of Christian clergywomen and the rigors that come with commitment to religious life, representing fourteen denominations as well as dozens of seminaries and colleges. 6 x 9, 240 pp, Quality PB, 978-1-59473-588-2 **$18.99**

She Lives! Sophia Wisdom Works in the World
By Rev. Jann Aldredge-Clanton, PhD
Fascinating narratives of clergy and laypeople who are changing the institutional church and society by restoring biblical female divine names and images to Christian theology, worship symbolism and liturgical language.
6 x 9, 320 pp, Quality PB, 978-1-59473-573-8 **$18.99**

Birthing God: Women's Experiences of the Divine
By Lana Dalberg; Foreword by Kathe Schaaf
Powerful narratives of suffering, love and hope that inspire both personal and collective transformation. 6 x 9, 304 pp, Quality PB, 978-1-59473-480-9 **$18.99**

Women, Spirituality and Transformative Leadership
Where Grace Meets Power
Edited by Kathe Schaaf, Kay Lindahl, Kathleen S. Hurty, PhD, and Reverend Guo Cheen
A dynamic conversation on the power of women's spiritual leadership and its emerging patterns of transformation.
6 x 9, 288 pp, Quality PB, 978-1-59473-548-6 **$18.99**; HC, 978-1-59473-313-0 **$24.99**

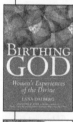

Spiritually Healthy Divorce: Navigating Disruption with Insight & Hope
By Carolyne Call A spiritual map to help you move through the twists and turns of divorce. 6 x 9, 224 pp, Quality PB, 978-1-59473-288-1 **$16.99**

Bread, Body, Spirit: Finding the Sacred in Food
Edited and with Introductions by Alice Peck 6 x 9, 224 pp, Quality PB, 978-1-59473-242-3 **$19.99**

Dance—The Sacred Art: The Joy of Movement as a Spiritual Practice
By Cynthia Winton-Henry 5½ x 8½, 224 pp, Quality PB, 978-1-59473-268-3 **$16.99**

Daughters of the Desert: Stories of Remarkable Women from Christian, Jewish and Muslim Traditions *By Claire Rudolf Murphy, Meghan Nuttall Sayres, Mary Cronk Farrell, Sarah Conover and Betsy Wharton*
5½ x 8½, 192 pp, Illus., Quality PB, 978-1-59473-106-8 **$16.99** Inc. reader's discussion guide

The Divine Feminine in Biblical Wisdom Literature
Selections Annotated & Explained
Translation & Annotation by Rabbi Rami Shapiro; Foreword by Rev. Cynthia Bourgeault, PhD
5½ x 8½, 240 pp, Quality PB, 978-1-59473-109-9 **$18.99**

Divining the Body: Reclaim the Holiness of Your Physical Self
By Jan Phillips 8 x 8, 256 pp, Quality PB, 978-1-59473-080-1 **$18.99**

Honoring Motherhood: Prayers, Ceremonies & Blessings
Edited and with Introductions by Lynn L. Caruso
5 x 7¼, 272 pp, Quality PB, 978-1-58473-384-0 **$9.99**; HC, 978-1-59473-239-3 **$19.99**

New Feminist Christianity: Many Voices, Many Views
Edited by Mary E. Hunt and Diann L. Neu
6 x 9, 384 pp, Quality PB, 978-1-59473-435-9 **$19.99**; HC, 978-1-59473-285-0 **$24.99**

Next to Godliness: Finding the Sacred in Housekeeping
Edited by Alice Peck 6 x 9, 224 pp, Quality PB, 978-1-59473-214-0 **$19.99**

The Triumph of Eve & Other Subversive Bible Tales
By Matt Biers-Ariel 5½ x 8½, 192 pp, Quality PB, 978-1-59473-176-1 **$14.99**

Woman Spirit Awakening in Nature: Growing Into the Fullness of Who You Are
By Nancy Barrett Chickerneo, PhD; Foreword by Eileen Fisher
8 x 8, 224 pp, b/w illus., Quality PB, 978-1-59473-250-8 **$16.99**

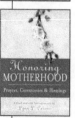

Women of Color Pray: Voices of Strength, Faith, Healing, Hope and Courage
Edited and with Introductions by Christal M. Jackson 5 x 7¼, 208 pp, Quality PB, 978-1-59473-077-1 **$15.99**

Spiritual Practice—The Sacred Art of Living Series

Teaching—The Sacred Art: The Joy of Opening Minds & Hearts
By Rev. Jane E. Vennard Explores the elements that make teaching a sacred art, recognizing it as a call to service rather than a job, and a vocation rather than a profession. 5½ x 8½, 160 pp, Quality PB, 978-1-59473-585-1 **$16.99**

Conversation—The Sacred Art: Practicing Presence in an Age of Distraction
By Diane M. Millis, PhD; Foreword by Rev. Tilden Edwards, PhD
5½ x 8½, 192 pp, Quality PB, 978-1-59473-474-8 **$16.99**

Dance—The Sacred Art: The Joy of Movement as a Spiritual Practice
By Cynthia Winton-Henry 5½ x 8½, 224 pp, Quality PB, 978-1-59473-268-3 **$16.99**

Dreaming—The Sacred Art: Incubating, Navigating & Interpreting Sacred
Dreams for Spiritual & Personal Growth By Lori Joan Swick, PhD
5½ x 8½, 224 pp, Quality PB, 978-1-59473-544-8 **$16.99**

Fly-Fishing—The Sacred Art: Casting a Fly as a Spiritual Practice
By Rabbi Eric Eisenkramer and Rev. Michael Attas, MD; Foreword by Chris Wood, CEO,
Trout Unlimited; Preface by Lori Simon, executive director, Casting for Recovery
5½ x 8½, 160 pp, Quality PB, 978-1-59473-299-7 **$16.99**

Giving—The Sacred Art: Creating a Lifestyle of Generosity
By Lauren Tyler Wright 5½ x 8½, 208 pp, Quality PB, 978-1-59473-224-9 **$16.99**

Haiku—The Sacred Art: A Spiritual Practice in Three Lines
By Margaret D. McGee 5½ x 8½, 192 pp, Quality PB, 978-1-59473-269-0 **$16.99**

Hospitality—The Sacred Art: Discovering the Hidden Spiritual Power of
Invitation and Welcome By Rev. Nanette Sawyer; Foreword by Rev. Dirk Ficca
5½ x 8½, 208 pp, Quality PB, 978-1-59473-228-7 **$16.99**

Labyrinths from the Outside In, 2nd Edition
Walking to Spiritual Insight—A Beginner's Guide By Rev. Dr. Donna Schaper and
Rev. Dr. Carole Ann Camp 6 x 9, 208 pp, b/w illus. and photos, Quality PB, 978-1-59473-486-1 **$16.99**

Lectio Divina—**The Sacred Art**
Transforming Words & Images into Heart-Centered Prayer
By Christine Valters Paintner, PhD 5½ x 8½, 240 pp, Quality PB, 978-1-59473-300-0 **$16.99**

Pilgrimage—The Sacred Art: Journey to the Center of the Heart
By Dr. Sheryl A. Kujawa-Holbrook 5½ x 8½, 240 pp, Quality PB, 978-1-59473-472-4 **$16.99**

Practicing the Sacred Art of Listening
A Guide to Enrich Your Relationships and Kindle Your Spiritual Life
By Kay Lindahl 8 x 8, 176 pp, Quality PB, 978-1-893361-85-0 **$18.99**

Recovery—The Sacred Art: The Twelve Steps as Spiritual Practice By Rami Shapiro
Foreword by Joan Borysenko, PhD 5½ x 8½, 240 pp, Quality PB, 978-1-59473-259-1 **$16.99**

Running—The Sacred Art: Preparing to Practice By Dr. Warren A. Kay
Foreword by Kristin Armstrong 5½ x 8½, 160 pp, Quality PB, 978-1-59473-227-0 **$16.99**

The Sacred Art of Chant: Preparing to Practice
By Ana Hernández 5½ x 8½, 192 pp, Quality PB, 978-1-59473-036-8 **$16.99**

The Sacred Art of Fasting: Preparing to Practice
By Thomas Ryan, CSP 5½ x 8½, 192 pp, Quality PB, 978-1-59473-078-8 **$15.99**

The Sacred Art of Forgiveness: Forgiving Ourselves and Others through God's Grace
By Marcia Ford 8 x 8, 176 pp, Quality PB, 978-1-59473-175-4 **$18.99**

The Sacred Art of Listening: Forty Reflections for Cultivating a Spiritual Practice
By Kay Lindahl; Illus. by Amy Schnapper 8 x 8, 160 pp, b/w illus., Quality PB, 978-1-893361-44-7 **$16.99**

The Sacred Art of Lovingkindness: Preparing to Practice
By Rabbi Rami Shapiro; Foreword by Marcia Ford 5½ x 8½, 176 pp, Quality PB, 978-1-59473-151-8 **$16.99**

Spiritual Adventures in the Snow: Skiing & Snowboarding as Renewal for Your Soul
By Dr. Marcia McFee and Rev. Karen Foster; Foreword by Paul Arthur
5½ x 8½, 208 pp, Quality PB, 978-1-59473-270-6 **$16.99**

Thanking & Blessing—The Sacred Art: Spiritual Vitality through Gratefulness
By Jay Marshall, PhD; Foreword by Philip Gulley 5½ x 8½, 176 pp, Quality PB, 978-1-59473-231-7 **$16.99**

Writing—The Sacred Art: Beyond the Page to Spiritual Practice
By Rami Shapiro and Aaron Shapiro 5½ x 8½, 192 pp, Quality PB, 978-1-59473-372-7 **$16.99**

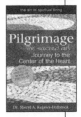

Sacred Texts—SkyLight Illuminations Series

Offers today's spiritual seeker an enjoyable entry into the great classic texts of the world's spiritual traditions. Each classic is presented in an accessible translation, with facing pages of guided commentary from experts, giving you the keys you need to understand the history, context and meaning of the text.

CHRISTIANITY

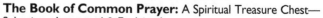

The Book of Common Prayer: A Spiritual Treasure Chest—Selections Annotated & Explained
Annotation by The Rev. Canon C. K. Robertson, PhD; Foreword by The Most Rev. Katharine Jefferts Schori; Preface by Archbishop Desmond Tutu
Makes available the riches of this spiritual treasure chest for all who are interested in deepening their life of prayer, building stronger relationships and making a difference in their world. 5½ x 8½, 208 pp, Quality PB, 978-1-59473-524-0 **$16.99**

Celtic Christian Spirituality: Essential Writings—Annotated & Explained
Annotation by Mary C. Earle; Foreword by John Philip Newell
Explores how the writings of this lively tradition embody the gospel.
5½ x 8½, 176 pp, Quality PB, 978-1-59473-302-4 **$16.99**

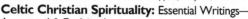

Desert Fathers and Mothers: Early Christian Wisdom Sayings—Annotated & Explained *Annotation by Christine Valters Paintner, PhD*
Opens up wisdom of the desert fathers and mothers for readers with no previous knowledge of Western monasticism and early Christianity.
5½ x 8½, 192 pp, Quality PB, 978-1-59473-373-4 **$16.99**

The End of Days: Essential Selections from Apocalyptic Texts—Annotated & Explained *Annotation by Robert G. Clouse, PhD*
Helps you understand the complex Christian visions of the end of the world.
5½ x 8¼, 224 pp, Quality PB, 978-1-59473-170-9 **$16.99**

The Hidden Gospel of Matthew: Annotated & Explained
Translation & Annotation by Ron Miller
Discover the words and events that have the strongest connection to the historical Jesus.
5½ x 8½, 272 pp, Quality PB, 978-1-59473-038-2 **$16.99**

The Imitation of Christ: Selections Annotated & Explained
Annotation by Paul Wesley Chilcote, PhD; By Thomas à Kempis; Adapted from John Wesley's The Christian's Pattern
Let Jesus's example of holiness, humility and purity of heart be a companion on your own spiritual journey.
5½ x 8½, 224 pp, Quality PB, 978-1-59473-434-2 **$16.99**

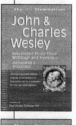

The Infancy Gospels of Jesus: Apocryphal Tales from the Childhoods of Mary and Jesus—Annotated & Explained
Translation & Annotation by Stevan Davies; Foreword by A. Edward Siecienski, PhD
A startling presentation of the early lives of Mary, Jesus and other biblical figures that will amuse and surprise you. 5½ x 8½, 176 pp, Quality PB, 978-1-59473-258-4 **$16.99**

John & Charles Wesley: Selections from Their Writings and Hymns—Annotated & Explained *Annotation by Paul W. Chilcote, PhD*
A unique presentation of the writings of these two inspiring brothers brings together some of the most essential material from their large corpus of work.
5½ x 8½, 288 pp, Quality PB, 978-1-59473-309-3 **$16.99**

Julian of Norwich: Selections from *Revelations of Divine Love*—Annotated & Explained *Annotation by Mary C. Earle; Foreword by Roberta C. Bondi*
Addresses topics including the infinite nature of God, the life of prayer, God's suffering with us, the eternal and undying life of the soul, the motherhood of Jesus and the motherhood of God and more.
5½ x 8½, 224 pp, Quality PB, 978-1-59473-513-4 **$16.99**

Sacred Texts—continued

CHRISTIANITY—continued

The Lost Sayings of Jesus: Teachings from Ancient Christian, Jewish, Gnostic and Islamic Sources—Annotated & Explained
Translation & Annotation by Andrew Phillip Smith; Foreword by Stephan A. Hoeller
Depicts Jesus as a Wisdom teacher who speaks to people of all faiths as a mystic and spiritual master. 5½ x 8½, 240 pp, Quality PB, 978-1-59473-172-3 **$16.99**

Philokalia: The Eastern Christian Spiritual Texts—Selections
Annotated & Explained *Annotation by Allyne Smith; Translation by G. E. H. Palmer, Phillip Sherrard and Bishop Kallistos Ware* The first approachable introduction to the wisdom of the Philokalia. 5½ x 8½, 240 pp, Quality PB, 978-1-59473-103-7 **$18.99**

The Sacred Writings of Paul: Selections Annotated & Explained
Translation & Annotation by Ron Miller Leads you into the exciting immediacy of Paul's teachings. 5½ x 8½, 224 pp, Quality PB, 978-1-59473-213-3 **$16.99**

Saint Augustine of Hippo: Selections from *Confessions* and Other Essential Writings—Annotated & Explained
Annotation by Joseph T. Kelley, PhD; Translation by the Augustinian Heritage Institute
Provides insight into the mind and heart of this foundational Christian figure.
5½ x 8½, 272 pp, Quality PB, 978-1-59473-282-9 **$18.99**

Saint Ignatius Loyola—The Spiritual Writings: Selections
Annotated & Explained *Annotation by Mark Mossa, SJ* Focuses on the practical mysticism of Ignatius of Loyola. 5½ x 8½, 288 pp, Quality PB, 978-1-59473-301-7 **$18.99**

Sex Texts from the Bible: Selections Annotated & Explained
Translation & Annotation by Teresa J. Hornsby; Foreword by Amy-Jill Levine
Demystifies the Bible's ideas on gender roles, marriage, sexual orientation, virginity, lust and sexual pleasure. 5½ x 8½, 208 pp, Quality PB, 978-1-59473-217-1 **$16.99**

Spiritual Writings on Mary: Annotated & Explained
Annotation by Mary Ford-Grabowsky; Foreword by Andrew Harvey
Examines the role of Mary, the mother of Jesus, as a source of inspiration in history and in life today. 5½ x 8½, 272 pp, Quality PB, 978-1-59473-001-6 **$16.99**

The Way of a Pilgrim: The Jesus Prayer Journey—Annotated &
Explained *Translation & Annotation by Gleb Pokrovsky; Foreword by Andrew Harvey* A classic of Russian Orthodox spirituality. 5½ x 8½, 160 pp, Illus., Quality PB, 978-1-893361-31-7 **$15.99**

GNOSTICISM

Gnostic Writings on the Soul: Annotated & Explained
Translation & Annotation by Andrew Phillip Smith; Foreword by Stephan A. Hoeller
Reveals the inspiring ways your soul can remember and return to its unique, divine purpose. 5½ x 8½, 144 pp, Quality PB, 978-1-59473-220-1 **$16.99**

The Gospel of Philip: Annotated & Explained
Translation & Annotation by Andrew Phillip Smith; Foreword by Stevan Davies
Reveals otherwise unrecorded sayings of Jesus and fragments of Gnostic mythology.
5½ x 8½, 160 pp, Quality PB, 978-1-59473-111-2 **$16.99**

The Gospel of Thomas: Annotated & Explained
Translation & Annotation by Stevan Davies; Foreword by Andrew Harvey
Sheds new light on the origins of Christianity and portrays Jesus as a wisdom-loving sage.
5½ x 8½, 192 pp, Quality PB, 978-1-893361-45-4 **$16.99**

The Secret Book of John: The Gnostic Gospel—Annotated & Explained
Translation & Annotation by Stevan Davies The most significant and influential text of the ancient Gnostic religion. 5½ x 8½, 208 pp, Quality PB, 978-1-59473-082-5 **$18.99**

See Inspiration for *Perennial Wisdom for the Spiritually Independent: Sacred Teachings—Annotated & Explained*

Spirituality

Mere Spirituality
The Spiritual Life According to Henri Nouwen
By Wil Hernandez, PhD, Obl. OSB; Foreword by Ronald Rolheiser

Introduction to Nouwen's spiritual thought, distills key insights on the realm of the spiritual life into one concise and compelling overview of his spirituality of the heart.

6 x 9, 160 pp (est), Quality PB, 978-1-59473-586-8 **$16.99**

The Forgiveness Handbook
Spiritual Wisdom and Practice for the Journey to Freedom, Healing and Peace
Created by the Editors at SkyLight Paths; Introduction by The Rev. Canon Marianne Wells Borg

Offers inspiration, encouragement and spiritual practice from across faith traditions for all who seek hope, wholeness and the freedom that comes from true forgiveness.

6 x 9, 256 pp, Quality PB, 978-1-59473-577-6 **$18.99**

Like a Child
Restoring the Awe, Wonder, Joy and Resiliency of the Human Spirit
By Rev. Timothy J. Mooney

By breaking free from our misperceptions about what it means to be an adult, we can reshape our world and become harbingers of grace. This unique spiritual resource explores Jesus's counsel to become like children in order to enter the kingdom of God. 6 x 9, 160 pp, Quality PB, 978-1-59473-543-1 **$16.99**

The Passionate Jesus: What We Can Learn from Jesus about Love, Fear, Grief, Joy and Living Authentically
By The Rev. Peter Wallace

Reveals Jesus as a passionate figure who was involved, present, connected, honest and direct with others and encourages you to build personal authenticity in every area of your own life. 6 x 9, 208 pp, Quality PB, 978-1-59473-393-2 **$18.99**

Gathering at God's Table: The Meaning of Mission in the Feast of Faith
By Katharine Jefferts Schori

A profound reminder of our role in the larger frame of God's dream for a restored and reconciled world. 6 x 9, 256 pp, HC, 978-1-59473-316-1 **$21.99**

The Heartbeat of God: Finding the Sacred in the Middle of Everything
By Katharine Jefferts Schori; Foreword by Joan Chittister, OSB

Explores our connections to other people, to other nations and with the environment through the lens of faith.

6 x 9, 240 pp, HC, 978-1-59473-292-8 **$21.99**; Quality PB, 978-1-59473-589-9 **$16.99**

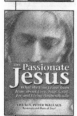

Laugh Your Way to Grace: Reclaiming the Spiritual Power of Humor
By Rev. Susan Sparks

A powerful, humorous case for laughter as a spiritual, healing path.

6 x 9, 176 pp, Quality PB, 978-1-59473-280-5 **$16.99**

Claiming Earth as Common Ground: The Ecological Crisis through the Lens of Faith
By Andrea Cohen-Kiener; Foreword by Rev. Sally Bingham
6 x 9, 192 pp, Quality PB, 978-1-59473-261-4 **$16.99**

Living into Hope: A Call to Spiritual Action for Such a Time as This
By Rev. Dr. Joan Brown Campbell; Foreword by Karen Armstrong
6 x 9, 208 pp, Quality PB, 978-1-59473-436-6 **$18.99**; HC, 978-1-59473-283-6 **$21.99**

Renewal in the Wilderness
A Spiritual Guide to Connecting with God in the Natural World
By John Lionberger 6 x 9, 176 pp, b/w photos, Quality PB, 978-1-59473-219-5 **$16.99**

A Walk with Four Spiritual Guides: Krishna, Buddha, Jesus, and Ramakrishna
By Andrew Harvey 5½ x 8½, 192 pp, b/w photos & illus., Quality PB, 978-1-59473-138-9 **$18.99**

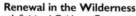

Prayer / Meditation

Calling on God
Inclusive Christian Prayers for Three Years of Sundays
By Peter Bankson and Deborah Sokolove
Prayers for today's world, vividly written for Christians who long for a way to talk to and about God that feels fresh yet still connected to tradition.
6 x 9, 400 pp, Quality PB, 978-1-59473-568-4 **$18.99**

The Worship Leader's Guide to Calling on God
8½ x 11, 20 pp, PB, 978-1-59473-591-2 **$9.99**

Openings, 2nd Edition
A Daybook of Saints, Sages, Psalms and Prayer Practices
By Rev. Larry J. Peacock
For anyone hungry for a richer prayer life, this prayer book offers daily inspiration to help you move closer to God. Draws on a wide variety of resources—lives of saints and sages from every age, psalms, and suggestions for personal reflection and practice. 6 x 9, 448 pp, Quality PB, 978-1-59473-545-5 **$18.99**

Openings: A Daybook of Saints, Sages, Psalms and Prayer Practices—Leader's Guide 8½ x 11, 12 pp, PB, 978-1-59473-572-1 **$9.99**

Men Pray: Voices of Strength, Faith, Healing, Hope and Courage
Created by the Editors at SkyLight Paths; With Introductions by Brian D. McLaren
Celebrates the rich variety of ways men around the world have called out to the Divine—with words of joy, praise, gratitude, wonder, petition and even anger—from the ancient world up to our own day.
5 x 7¼, 192 pp, HC, 978-1-59473-395-6 **$16.99**

Honest to God Prayer: Spirituality as Awareness, Empowerment, Relinquishment and Paradox *By Kent Ira Groff*
6 x 9, 192 pp, Quality PB, 978-1-59473-433-5 **$16.99**

Lectio Divina—The Sacred Art
Transforming Words & Images into Heart-Centered Prayer
By Christine Valters Paintner, PhD
5½ x 8½, 240 pp, Quality PB, 978-1-59473-300-0 **$16.99**

Sacred Attention: A Spiritual Practice for Finding God in the Moment
By Margaret D. McGee 6 x 9, 144 pp, Quality PB, 978-1-59473-291-1 **$16.99**

Secrets of Prayer: A Multifaith Guide to Creating Personal Prayer in Your Life
By Nancy Corcoran, CSJ 6 x 9, 160 pp, Quality PB, 978-1-59473-215-7 **$16.99**

Women of Color Pray: Voices of Strength, Faith, Healing, Hope and Courage
Edited and with Introductions by Christal M. Jackson
5 x 7¼, 208 pp, Quality PB, 978-1-59473-077-1 **$15.99**

Prayer / M. Basil Pennington, OCSO

Finding Grace at the Center, 3rd Edition: The Beginning of Centering Prayer *With Thomas Keating, OCSO, and Thomas E. Clarke, SJ*
Foreword by Rev. Cynthia Bourgeault, PhD A practical guide to a simple and beautiful form of meditative prayer. 5 x 7¼, 128 pp, Quality PB, 978-1-59473-182-2 **$12.99**

The Monks of Mount Athos: A Western Monk's Extraordinary Spiritual Journey on Eastern Holy Ground *Foreword by Archimandrite Dionysios*
Explores the landscape, monastic communities and food of Athos.
6 x 9, 352 pp, Quality PB, 978-1-893361-78-2 **$18.95**

Psalms: A Spiritual Commentary *Illus. by Phillip Ratner*
Reflections on some of the most beloved passages from the Bible's most widely read book. 6 x 9, 176 pp, 24 full-page b/w illus., Quality PB, 978-1-59473-234-8 **$16.99**

The Song of Songs: A Spiritual Commentary *Illus. by Phillip Ratner*
Explore the Bible's most challenging mystical text.
6 x 9, 160 pp, 14 full-page b/w illus., Quality PB, 978-1-59473-235-5 **$16.99**
HC, 978-1-59473-004-7 **$19.99**

About SKYLIGHT PATHS Publishing

SkyLight Paths Publishing is creating a place where people of different spiritual traditions come together for challenge and inspiration, a place where we can help each other understand the mystery that lies at the heart of our existence.

Through spirituality, our religious beliefs are increasingly becoming a part of our lives—rather than *apart* from our lives. While many of us may be more interested than ever in spiritual growth, we may be less firmly planted in traditional religion. Yet, we do want to deepen our relationship to the sacred, to learn from our own as well as from other faith traditions, and to practice in new ways.

SkyLight Paths sees both believers and seekers as a community that increasingly transcends traditional boundaries of religion and denomination—people wanting to learn from each other, *walking together, finding the way.*

For your information and convenience, at the back of this book we have provided a list of other SkyLight Paths books you might find interesting and useful. They cover the following subjects:

Buddhism / Zen	Gnosticism	Poetry
Catholicism	Hinduism /	Prayer
Chaplaincy	Vedanta	Religious Etiquette
Children's Books	Inspiration	Retirement & Later-
Christianity	Islam / Sufism	Life Spirituality
Comparative	Judaism	Spiritual Biography
Religion	Meditation	Spiritual Direction
Earth-Based	Mindfulness	Spirituality
Spirituality	Monasticism	Women's Interest
Enneagram	Mysticism	Worship
Global Spiritual	Personal Growth	
Perspectives		

Or phone, mail or email to: SKYLIGHT PATHS Publishing
An imprint of Turner Publishing Company
4507 Charlotte Avenue • Suite 100 • Nashville, Tennessee 37209
Tel: (615) 255-2665 • www.skylightpaths.com
Prices subject to change.